A. Seeker's Storybook

Stories for the Working Soul

by Michelle Tocher

WonderLit Press

Copyright © 2000, 2016 by Michelle Tocher

All rights reserved. No part of this book may be reproduced in any form without permission in writing from the author.

ISBN 978-0-9738776-3-2

Published by WonderLit Press, Toronto, ON, 2016

Reprint. Originally published by The Canadian Career Development Foundation (CCDF), Ottawa, Canada, 2000.

Illustrations by Richard Leach

Table of Contents

DEDICATION 5

FROM THE DESK OF A. SEEKER.. 6

CHAPTER 1: Changes... 9
    The Mountain Change 13

CHAPTER 2: Under Control.. 17
    The Thought-Con Troll 21

CHAPTER 3: Meeting a Heroine.. 31
    The Rag Dolls 35

CHAPTER 4: Call to Adventure.. 43
    The Permanent Cat 47

CHAPTER 5: Finding the Orphan... 51
    The Orphan 56

CHAPTER 6: Leap to Freedom... 63
    The Butterflower 66

CHAPTER 7: The Wild Side... 69
    Seafood Special 72

CHAPTER 8: Waiting... 79
    The Broken Pot 82

CHAPTER 9: Seeing the Treasure Within 89
    The Treasures of the Mine 93

CHAPTER 10: Getting Naked..101
    Old Woman's Hill 104

CHAPTER 11: Down to the Core 109
    The Divided Man 113

CHAPTER 12: Dream Fields...119
    The Flammable Angel 122

CHAPTER 13: Coming to Light...129
    The Oyster's Gift 132

CHAPTER 14: Playing it Out 137
    THAT Place 139

CHAPTER 15: The Big Test 147
    Starry Eyes 151

CHAPTER 16: Full Circle 155
    The Broad Mind 159

EPILOGUE 165

ABOUT THE AUTHOR AND ILLUSTRATOR 166

For my sister, Jackie, who is the rose in our garden

FROM THE DESK OF A. SEEKER

To: *YOU*
Subject: *The Storybook*

At last I'm sending you the collection of stories that have meant so much to me over the last few years. They came along at a time of great upheaval and radically shifted the way I look at my work and my life.

In the beginning I was just your average working stiff. I had a job in the media department of an insurance company, and, like everybody else around me, I did my job with certain assumptions. I expected that if you're loyal, competent and hardworking, the company will be loyal to you, and you'll grow together over time.

Then, out of the blue, changes started happening. Management sent out notices of an upcoming merger, which was followed by a reengineering of systems and a sweeping restructuring of our departments. New people came in and heads began to roll.

Needless to say, the friendly atmosphere of the company changed. People became suspicious, competitive, and sometimes downright nasty. The ones who were "made redundant" felt betrayed, and those of us who were left behind had to work twice as hard with no reassurance that any of our efforts would be rewarded. We'd be lucky if we kept our jobs.

Strangely enough, this crazy, disruptive, depressing time also turned out to be a very positive shakeup for me. I started questioning my expectations and beliefs about the meaning of work—and life, for that matter. As I did, stories started showing up. They weren't your usual reenactments of daily life. They were mythic stories—fables, you might call them—that mirrored my deeper experience. The odd thing was that I would find a story (or the story would find me) right at the time I needed it. As I read it I would think, "That is exactly what I'm going through!"

Over the course of three years, those magical mystery stories kept me on track, gave me perspective, changed my thinking and made me laugh. They opened me up to possibilities I'd never considered before. I started digging into my inner resources to find what I felt called to do. I'm no rocket scientist but I'm convinced that we've all got something unique to offer that comes with a special set of gifts.

What I have done here is to compile my journal entries with the stories that came to me as I went through the changes. I found that if I took some time to reflect on an image from the story, if I literally drew it out, I would get a surprising insight. That's something you might want to do as you go through the book. Just sit a while with something that speaks to you, and see what comes up.

That's all for now. Enjoy the storybook! I hope you find some gold.

Yours truly,

Albert Seeker

CHAPTER 1

Changes

CHAPTER 1: Changes

A Seeker's Journal

September 4

It's getting almost impossible to work these days. There have been so many layoffs in our department, we're getting buzz-bombed every few months. Down here in the trenches we're shell-shocked, and above ground, the generals aren't providing much in the way of intelligence.

I'm working in the media production department of an insurance company called Commercial Life. Or rather, I'm trying to work. There used to be four people in our department. Now there's only a coordinator, and that's me. I don't know who my boss is anymore. Demands are flying at me from all directions, and, like everyone else on our floor, I'm working harder than ever just to survive. Morale is nil. My doctor suggested that I get some massage therapy for my headaches, so I went the other day, and I asked the guy, "How am I doing?" And he said, "Well, lemme see. You're shouldering a big load, gritting your teeth, breaking your back, swallowing your pride, girding your loins, and holding on for dear life."

I'm not dealing with this very well. My headaches are getting worse. I'm grinding my teeth at night. I really want to hold onto this job. I fought so hard to get here in the first place. I don't even want to think about what I'll do if I lose it. Where will I go?

What really demoralizes me is the feeling that slowly but surely, we're all being replaced by machines. Connie, the administrative assistant for our production department, got laid off last week. We now have a completely automated reception service. We're supposed to forget Connie, like that's possible. No machine could replace her spirit, her sense of humour, her wit, and her ability to level with anyone no matter what their position. All that went away with Connie and I'd like to see a machine replace that.

It's late. I should stop writing. I'm depressing myself. The fact is, I'm trying to survive the best way I can. I'm reading a lot of inspirational books these days; trying to get some sort of perspective on what's going on, what all this change means and how we're being challenged by it. I'm especially interested in mythology and storytelling. There was a time when the storyteller played a vital role in the community. People listened to stories to find out about themselves: who they were, where they came from, where they were going. I read somewhere that when TV was first introduced to a tribe in Africa, the people got all excited, and for a couple of weeks all they did was watch TV. But then they forgot about it and went back to their old storyteller.

CHAPTER 1: Changes

The visiting anthropologist who saw this was confused, so he asked one of the villagers, "Don't you think the TV knows more stories than your old storyteller?" The fellow replied, "Oh yes, the TV knows more stories, but the storyteller knows ME!"

What does the storyteller know about me? Who can explain what these changes mean?

CHAPTER 1: Changes

FROM THE DESK OF A. SEEKER

I found this story, "The Mountain Change," in a newsletter that was lying around in the coffee room at the office. It struck me right away because it drew such a vivid picture of radical change—and on some deep level it seemed to address my question: "What do these changes mean?"

CHAPTER 1: Changes

The Mountain Change

Once upon a time, there was a mountain range called the Change Range. It boasted the highest peaks in the world, and went all the way around the earth.

The people who lived on the slopes of Change were better adapted than anyone else in the world, because the mountain constantly rose and fell. They might go to bed at night in a deep valley and wake up the next morning on a high alpine ridge. As a result, the mountain people knew how to survive in any climate, at any altitude, and they were happy with their lot.

But then one day a terrible thing happened—the whole mountain range exploded! It spewed fire into the air, sending rivers of molten rock down to the valley. The earth quaked and split. Houses were torn apart and people were thrown off the mountain, hurled off ridges and swallowed up into the fiery abyss.

Those who survived fled the roaring mountain, leaving everything behind. They ran across the plain, across rivers and through forests until they reached a place of safety. Then, as the sun set, they stood on a hill and looked back at the mountain.

They couldn't believe their eyes, for the whole range was moving. It slithered and it wound from side to side like a snake. They realized that this was no mountain. It was a dragon! It shook and roared, sending tremors around the earth, casting off centuries of soil, growth and trees. In the setting sun, the dragon's green scales shimmered like malachite, and the high, craggy peaks of its spines shone like gold.

The people tried to make sense of what they saw. What did it mean? If the mountain range went around the earth, then the earth must belong, not to the people, but to the dragon. The dragon must have been sleeping. That would explain why the mountain shifted from time to time, and rose and fell at predictable intervals. But now it had awoken! Everything they had constructed—their buildings, their ideas, their science—collapsed with this new event.

"What is it doing here?" the people asked. But they had no answers. They only knew that nothing would ever be the same. The earth might be the dragon's EGG for all they knew.

An old, old woman named Mrs. Chang sat on a rock and looked back at the faces of the people who stood all in a row on the hill, staring at the mountain. Some looked at the dragon with wonder, others covered their eyes, some covered their children's eyes. Some were concerned, others puzzled, others excited. The whole range of human emotion played on a whole range of faces, young and old.

CHAPTER 1: Changes

Now, some people returned to the mountain. Mrs. Chang was one of them. They had not lost the ancient stories about the origins of the mountain range. They began to gather together, collect the legends, and learn how people had lived on the mountain before the dragon went to sleep. Slowly they adapted to the mountain's movements, as their ancestors had done. They learned to "ride on the back of the dragon," as old Mrs. Chang would say, and the dragon did provide.

Meanwhile, the people on the plains lived in constant fear. They never knew where the dragon was going to move next, so no one ever felt safe. As time went by, some of the plains folk decided to go back to the mountain in search of lost roots and loved ones. It took a great deal of courage to make the journey, but when they did, they were amazed to find that the mountain people had adapted and were making a livelihood in this new, fluid and beautiful place.

Before too long, the lights of houses and towns appeared along the dragon's spiny ridge, all around the world, so the people on the plain could see where they needed to go if they wanted to stop living in fear.

Eventually everyone went to live on the back of the dragon, and then, as time passed, the dragon grew quiet, and went back to sleep again ...

For now.

CHAPTER 1: Changes

CHAPTER 1: Changes

"The earth might be the dragon's EGG for all they knew."

I keep seeing this dragon coiled around the earth and I've been drawing it in a dozen ways. I'm like one of those observers who is standing on the hill stunned by the idea that the earth might be an EGG. Like Nature, the dragon is bigger than any of us. Is Nature indifferent? I used to think so. But maybe she's not. Maybe the earth is an egg that belongs to something out there in space, some intelligence that can see more of the plan. What if our science fiction stories are true? What if we're being watched and listened to? What if some big cosmic hen is monitoring our changes and waiting for the egg to crack?

I remember a dream I had not long ago. I was standing under the night sky, looking up at the stars. Beside me, to my left, stood a table, covered in a white cloth like an altar. On the table I saw a book, a candle and a packet of matches. I was supposed to perform a ritual in preparation for the arrival of some visitors, which I assumed were from outer space. The ceremony involved reading a passage from the book, striking a match, and lighting the candle. I was petrified. I didn't want to be there. The only relief the dream gave me was that if I totally lost it, I could pull the curtain behind the table and let in the daylight. So, I performed the ritual and right after I lit the candle, a fist burst out from inside of my body. I yelled like hell and woke up. My body in no uncertain terms said to me, "The change isn't coming from OUT THERE—it's coming from IN HERE."

Wow. It's not just the world that's changing. WE'RE changing. Something's hatching IN US.

CHAPTER 2

Under Control

CHAPTER 2: Under Control

A Seeker's Journal

September 25

This morning the communications director, Milton "The Cadaver" Cadwell, called me into his office. We call him "The Cadaver" because he's tall and ungainly, with abnormally white skin and a balding pate. He really could play a convincing role as Death the way he sits there on the other side of his desk in his gray suit and stares at you, pressing his fingers against one another like he's holding a pane of glass.

Cadwell is building his empire. Recently the media department has come under his control. I know he thinks I'm incompetent. I'm no great writer, but I can do a pretty decent storyboard and I've got a first rate team of outside writers and directors that I use. Everything I've produced is quality work. Cadwell never acknowledged that, and I didn't care until he took control. Now everything I do has to please him. I'm becoming a sniveling, hateful little brown-noser, and in turn all I get is his disapproval. He's tracking me and waiting for me to slip up. Just like Death.

So Cadwell said to me: "About that video you're working on for the product launch, I want you to do it in-house."

I balked. I tried to explain. First of all, I've already hired a team. We don't have a contract yet, but they've already done a lot of design on the strength of my word. My word has always been good. And second, we don't have the engine in-house. We've got ancient cameras and editing equipment. There's no way we could do a glitzy product launch video with our stuff. It's crazy. Even if I was Steven Spielberg it would bomb. All this I tried to explain.

Cadwell pressed his fingertips together, implacable. He said, "I want to show management what we can do. IN-HOUSE." He stared right through me with those steely blue eyes.

I stammered, "I can't pull it off."

"That would be unfortunate for you, Mr. Seeker."

I got up and left his office, slamming the door behind me. So this is it. So he's done it. He's not only going to fire me, he's going to humiliate me. Well I'm not going to give him the pleasure. I'm going to hold onto my team. I'll pay them with money from another budget. Hell, I'll borrow money and pay them out of my own pocket if I have to. I'm not following orders this time.

CHAPTER 2: Under Control

November 28

We launched the product. Played the video on a big screen to a room of about 200 brokers. A decent little flick if I don't say so myself. Management was impressed. The Cadaver didn't flinch, but I watched him from the sidelines and I saw his eyes get narrower and narrower. Then when everyone was applauding, he turned and shot me an icy look.

Yep. I'm a dead man.

FROM THE DESK OF A. SEEKER

"The Thought-Con Troll" was e-mailed to me by a friend who sends me interesting things from time to time. I hadn't told her about Cadwell, so the timing was pretty amazing ... especially as I had started to doubt my own sanity. The story affirmed to me that I had done the right thing. It gave me a perspective on what I was standing up to, and what I was standing FOR.

CHAPTER 2: Under Control

The Thought-Con Troll

One dark day, during a time when the world was inhabited by trolls, a girl named Maria was walking along a cobblestone road absorbed in her thoughts.

She thought about how much she loved to sew, and how lovely it would be to make the finest dresses in all the world, and the thought made her consider the idea of becoming a seamstress. She thought perhaps she might go and work for Mrs. Peabody, who had recently posted a "Help" sign on her door. She arrived at a picturesque little bridge that arched over a stream, and made her way across. Midway, she paused to look at the water.

Suddenly, a troll popped his head out from under the bridge.

"Stop that racket up there," he demanded. His skin was greenish and his beard was dripping with the river's slime. He wore an open red vest, green trousers, and his hands and feet were very large.

"What racket?" asked Maria.

"The racket of your thoughts," he snapped irritably. He stamped out from under the bridge and hopped up under the railing. Quick as a wink he stood before the girl, who was rather disconcerted to be suddenly affronted by this creature she had only read about in storybooks.

"Your thoughts are coming through loud and clear. This is my bridge and I'm not having any of them," said the troll, puffing out his hairy little chest. "It's a damnable invasion of my privacy, that's what it is," he continued.

"I didn't know this bridge belonged to you, sir. I'll just be on my way," said Maria, not wanting any conflict with the chap.

She must have said exactly what he wanted to hear, because his demeanor changed. He thrust his big green hands into his trouser pockets and assumed a conversational attitude.

"Let me give you a word of advice," he said. "Don't let yourself think your own thoughts, on my bridge or anywhere else."

"Why not?" asked Maria. She was very green herself, in a manner of speaking, since she'd only just finished her mother's apprenticeship and knew nothing of the ways of the world.

"Because it's the most dangerous thing you can do. You'll run into nothing but conflict your whole life long."

"Then whose thoughts should I think?" Maria asked.

CHAPTER 2: Under Control

"Why, the thoughts of the people ABOVE you," he replied, pulling a pipe out of his pocket and lighting it.

She considered this for a moment. "I see, the thoughts of the people I admire."

The troll stamped on the match and burned the underside of his foot. "No, no, no!" he shouted, grabbing his foot. "I'm not talking about the people you admire. I'm talking about the people in positions higher than your own."

"I see, people in higher positions."

"That's right. Exactly right," he said, puffing away on his pipe.

"Higher positions ..." she repeated.

"That's how you'll get up in the world," he said reassuringly.

"Well, thank you, sir, I'll remember that," she replied.

The troll returned to his home under the bridge and Maria set out to make her fortune in the world. She decided that since her mother thought she was a good seamstress, and her mother was certainly in a higher position than herself, the idea of going to see Mrs. Peabody was still a good one. Gathering her courage, she went directly to Mrs. Peabody's shop.

She rang the bell and found Mrs. Peabody at her desk writing in a large ledger under the glow of a little oil lamp.

"Mrs. Peabody? I see you have posted a sign for help."

Mrs. Peabody looked up over her eyeglasses. She pulled herself up from behind the desk and came towards Maria with her measuring tape dangling off her heavy bosom like a climber's rope.

For a moment Maria thought she was going to get measured, and well, Mrs. Peabody was certainly about to give the girl a measurement, only one of another kind.

"You're Mattie McCormick's girl, are you not?"

"Yes I am, ma'am. Maria, ma'am," she said, curtseying.

"Hhmn. So what can you do, young lady?" She studied the girl impatiently with her concentration focused on Maria's hands which were at the present time, turning in and out of one another nervously.

"My mother taught me to sew, ma'am. I believe I am very good at it. You see, since Mama lost her eyesight, I've made all the family's everyday clothes."

"How many's that again?"

CHAPTER 2: Under Control

"Eight children and three adults, ma'am, if you include Grandmama."

"You sewed the whole lot?"

"Oh, yes I did, trousers and blouses and dresses and undergarments and coats … and all the mending too … also Alicia's little doll clothes, with all their fine stitching. They were my favorite, Mrs. Peabody. I brought a sample so you can see the detail …." Maria dug into her bag.

"How many pairs of trousers can you make in a week?" Mrs. Peabody demanded. She took off her eyeglasses and put them on the desk.

"Oh, I would say at least one pair a day …."

Mrs. Peabody raised her heavy black eyebrows. "That's impressive, young lady."

"Yes, but it isn't nearly as impressive as all your work, Mrs. Peabody. I don't know anyone who wouldn't want to come to you for their fancy dresses. You make the finest fancy dresses in all the world! If only I could—"

"Bah, fancy dresses. They're going out of fashion, my dear. Put that thought out of your head." Mrs. Peabody waved off Maria's thought as though it were a bee.

"I'm sorry, Mrs. Peabody. I had no business thinking such thoughts."

"You certainly didn't, child," she sniffed.

Maria stammered, "I don't know why I had no business thinking, but …"

"Because this is MY business, and if you're going to work for me—"

"I should think YOUR thoughts," said Maria.

"Exactly," said Mrs. Peabody, satisfied.

She repositioned herself at her desk, licked her index finger and flipped through a stack of papers, counting numbers off to herself.

"You're hired," she said, after some time had passed.

Only a few days after Maria had started work, Mrs. Peabody came into the back room and found the girl sewing and humming to herself in the afternoon sun. Mrs. Peabody thrust a box of thread under her nose.

"This is not the thread I told you to buy," she said.

"Oh, it cost a little more, but—"

"It's not the thread I TOLD you to buy," Mrs. Peabody repeated harshly. Her face had gone bloodless and her complexion, very gray.

CHAPTER 2: Under Control

"The quality of the thread you told me to buy is poor. Begging your pardon ma'am, but it will break," said Maria. "I know because I've tried—"

"ENOUGH!" Mrs. Peabody bellowed. "I tell you what to buy, and I expect you to buy it." Mrs. Peabody was formidable today, though in truth, she wasn't an easygoing person on the best of days.

"But it will break!" exclaimed Maria.

"I WANT it to break, you stupid child!"

Maria was too astonished to say anything, so she began to cry.

"It's cheaper. The cheaper it is the less the clothes will cost, the more they'll wear and the more my customers will come in for repairs. That's business, and if you don't like it you shouldn't be in it. Now. You take this back."

"But that's not right, Mrs. Peabody," Maria blubbered.

"Don't you rile me now, girl, with your sentimental ideas. My heart's not good," said Mrs. Peabody, breathing with difficulty.

"But it isn't fair that we should take people's money, knowing full well their seams will split—"

Mrs. Peabody reeled and crashed to the floor, which nearly brought the old store down. Maria ran outside for help and the doctor came. He revived the old lady well enough to help her to her feet, and prescribed a week of bed rest. Dr. Browning gave Maria harsh words regarding the importance of diplomacy in the presence of humans with weak hearts.

Maria learned her lesson. She went out and exchanged the thread. She realized how right the troll had been. Not only would she cause trouble if she thought her own thoughts, she might even kill someone! No more, she vowed, never again, no matter what the cost, would she ever, ever, think her own thoughts.

Soon Mrs. Peabody recovered, and Maria's relationship with her boss improved considerably. Maria stepped into Mrs. Peabody's thoughts like she was stepping into her clothes. She ignored the poor quality of the fabric and the thread. Thrifty Mrs. Peabody narrowed all the seams and wasted nothing, and everywhere Maria turned, it seemed there was less and less give in the world. Certainly there was no room for fat, except on persons like Mrs. Peabody who seemed to grow fatter by the day.

Time passed, and Mrs. Peabody's operation grew by leaps and bounds. Maria now supervised a dozen farm girls and Mrs. Peabody stopped doing custom work altogether. Nothing was done to fit people, everything was sewn to fit a pattern.

CHAPTER 2: Under Control

"Divide and conquer," became Mrs. Peabody's favorite aphorism. Under her direction, Maria began segregating the girls into groups to cut patterns and groups to sew seams.

"Best put the ones who aren't friendly together," Mrs. Peabody advised. "They'll work harder."

Mrs. Peabody's factory produced an army of trousers, shirts, skirts and blouses that hung sullenly in rows on the rack at the end of the day. People would put their money down to buy them and wear them for a short time. Then the seams would split or the buttons would break and they would return to buy more. They never realized that Mrs. Peabody was behind it all with her good business sense.

Maria had no time to think about the big picture, however. Her attention was focused on the quota her girls had to fill. She became completely occupied with income and expenses, savings and profits. At night, her head pounded with thoughts of money, while her heart tightened to fight back the thoughts of betrayed friends and split seams.

One morning after many sleepless nights, Maria trudged to work. As she approached the bridge, the mist was coming off the water and the sky looked like a pearl bowl, lit from behind by a pale pink light. Maria didn't notice the sky or the mist, though. She was too exhausted and sore-hearted to notice anything. When she set foot on the bridge, she felt all the life drain out of her and she fell into a faint.

"I can't think Mrs. Peabody's thoughts anymore," she whimpered. "The thoughts I have are not my thoughts. I don't know what my own thoughts are anymore." Maria began to weep as though she had lost her best friend, as of course she had.

When she had emptied out all her tears and all Mrs. Peabody's thoughts, and indeed, all thoughts of every kind, she opened her eyes. The sun shone brightly over the river, causing the water to twinkle playfully. Maria's spirit recovered a little, and she noticed a furry caterpillar inching its way towards her.

Her first thought was to shoo the ghastly thing away. But no sooner did she think that thought, than she caught herself. "Now wait a minute," she said to herself. "Where did I get that thought that this little fellow is a horrible thing? Is that MY thought?"

"No, I don't think so!" She held out her right hand and let the caterpillar crawl up her arm. She noticed how steadily it made its way, so tirelessly and with such determination. He didn't worry about the future or fret because he hadn't yet become a butterfly. Suddenly she felt great affection for his singular charm.

"I think you are a beautiful creature," she announced. As if in reply, the creature rolled off her arm and onto the bridge.

CHAPTER 2: Under Control

Suddenly, joy bloomed in Maria. Everywhere she looked the world seemed fresh and new. She got to her feet and ran her fingers along the railing of the sturdy old bridge. "Who are you, bridge?" she asked. "When were you built? Who would have fashioned you so sturdy and with such care? Why, you are as beautiful as the dresses I would have made if I had fashioned them with my own thoughts instead of with Mrs. Peabody's!"

"Enough, enough!" shrieked the troll, scampering out from the underside of the bridge. "I will not have these thoughts on my bridge! Go home, go home, you troublemaker!"

Maria had failed to remember this particular feature of the bridge. She gathered up her courage.

"You, sir, told me to think the thoughts of the people who were higher than me. And I did. But after working for Mrs. Peabody, I would rather think my own thoughts."

"Fool!" yelled the troll, stamping around the bridge. Maria stared at the creature and tried to figure out how to turn the thought of him around. Finally, she asked: "How is it that you've come to live under this bridge, sir?"

The troll was taken aback, and then he said, "This is MY bridge. I've worked all my life to arrive at my position in the world."

"Is this where you have come to after a whole lifetime of work, sir? Begging your pardon, but I would think that a man like you would have found a better place to live than under a bridge, as beautiful as this old gray bridge is, I mean."

"Don't tell me about my lifetime of work!" he shrieked. Smoke began to escape from his ears and his eyes and his nose all at the same time. "See what happens when you think your own thoughts! See what you're doing to me? I've done very well for myself, thank you very much. So don't you try and make me see me. Don't you try, because I won't, I won't!" Tongues of fire licked out from his nostrils and his ears, and all of a sudden he burst into flames. In a moment, there was nothing left on the bridge but a pile of ash.

Maria's heart went out to the little troll because she realized what a frightened thing he was, and how good his original intention had been. He had, after all, only wished to please. She lay down on the bridge and stared at the little mound of ash, lost in her thoughts about the troll.

Her reverie was suddenly interrupted by a naked doll that dangled in front of her eyes. Clinging to the doll was a little girl of four with large brown eyes and curly brown hair. Holding the little girl's hand was her mother, who peered downward at Maria with a look of mild concern.

CHAPTER 2: Under Control

"She needs clothes," said Maria, pointing to the little girl's doll.

"She does indeed," said the mother, "And so do all the dolls in my store."

"Well, well," said Maria, "I do fine stitching."

The woman extended her hand to help Maria onto her feet, and the three started off to town.

CHAPTER 2: Under Control

CHAPTER 2: Under Control

"Don't you try and make me see me because I won't, I won't!"

I have spent some time playing and re-playing this scene in my head. Not because I want a feeling of revenge but because I want to keep remembering how sorry I feel for that little dude. He has worked so hard for his position in life. He doesn't want to see that he's an ugly heartless little bastard who lives under a bridge. I don't blame him for not wanting to see himself. It would be truly fatal. He's a creation of the world, after all. If he goes up in flames, what's left?

My Aunt Helen and her second husband Donald came over to the apartment for a drink the other day, en route south to their place in Florida. I'm in the kitchen fixing their gin and tonics and I can hear Helen saying, "You know, maybe we should try and rent the house while we're down there this year instead of doing it when we get back," and Donald snaps, "That's ridiculous, I'm not going to spend three months trying to find a tenant for the winter."

"I know, dear, but we couldn't rent it last year, and it's cutting into my nest egg. There are all kinds of real estate agencies that do this for people. I know because Elma ...." And Donald says, "I said no, and that's it." I came around with the drinks and there's Donald sitting in the middle of the sofa like a toad on a log. Another bloody troll. Where do they get off thinking that they can push everybody around? Why do we pander to their every need? Why don't we just come out with it and say, "Don't talk to me like that you fat old toad. Show me some respect!"

I'm glad I stood up to the Cadaver. I'm glad I didn't let him have his way. Let him fire me. It's going to happen anyway, sooner or later. It's only a matter of time—in the big picture, we're all going to die one day. But if I had sold out my principles before I got fired, where would I be then? I'd be nothing but troll ash.

CHAPTER 3

Meeting a Heroine

CHAPTER 3: Meeting a Heroine

A Seeker's Journal

January 29

Two weeks ago, Cadwell hired a woman named Caroline Marcos, a writer/producer, to run the media department: which means me. It seems management wants more in-house control and professional handling of their videos. I got wind of this from the communications department before Caroline showed up, and I admit, I was prepared to hate her. Patricia (a PR writer) found out that Caroline wasn't even hired as a full-time employee. She's here on contract, working a four-day week. She warned me, "You watch, she'll replace you." I'm thinking to myself, Why don't they just fire me? I know the answer. The Cadaver wants to make me experience my redundancy before making me redundant. He wants to watch me roast.

So, I'm sitting there in my cubicle, and in walks Caroline, this tall dark-haired beauty of Spanish descent with an hour glass figure and a truly generous smile. In spite of myself I liked her immediately. Here is a woman who knows herself. She doesn't wear the corporate suit. She has her own style. It's all about flow: long hair, dresses, sweaters, boots. I imagine she's in her early thirties somewhere. Right away, she sat down with me and wanted to know how I felt about having her around. She told me exactly what her arrangement with management was. I said I wasn't too happy about having her there but I had no choice other than to live with it. I acted pretty sullen but she was making me blush. I won't say I'm good looking. I'm sort of average height: mouse brown curly hair, blue eyes, somewhat fleshy nose. I wear my hair over my ears because they stick out of my head, and when I cut my hair I look too much like Alfred E. Neuman for my own comfort.

Anyway, I don't think appearance makes much of an impression on Caroline, although hers certainly does. I have to admit being somewhat amused by the stir she's creating in the communications department. She's become a source of gossip, an object of envy, a possible date. Everybody's trying to figure her out; fit her in. For her part, she hasn't shown an interest in anyone or anything outside the media department. She focuses on the job she was hired to do; cuts her own path, brings her own lunch. She reads screenwriting books at noon hour and dreams of writing a screenplay about the Romantic poets. She's a single mother with a seven-year-old son named Christopher, and when she isn't consulting or mothering, she's volunteering for a women's shelter. She told me a bit about herself the other day when we were having a coffee. Her view is that we're all heroes in our own story. She said: "It's a pretty good deal, huh? You get to play the lead and you don't even have to audition!"

I laughed. Then I said, "Yeah, but what if you don't want the lead? What if you would rather be an extra?"

CHAPTER 3: Meeting a Heroine

"You can't be," she replied, smirking. "Even if you think you're an extra, you're still playing the lead."

I'm beginning not to care that she's making me redundant, I just hope she'll inject me with enough of her thinking to sustain me in my joblessness.

CHAPTER 3: Meeting a Heroine

FROM THE DESK OF A. SEEKER

Carolina gave me this story, "The Rag Dolls," when I asked her to give me an example of someone she considered to be a hero. The last thing I expected from her was a story about DOLLS!

CHAPTER 3: Meeting a Heroine

The Rag Dolls

There is this little four year old boy named Danny, and Danny loves dolls. Everywhere he goes, he wants to take his dolls with him. He lives with his Mom and he doesn't have a Dad around to make a fuss about having dolls. His mother doesn't mind. She thinks it's kind of neat that Danny loves dolls, and she's given him all her own, along with a few from the bargain store. But mostly, Danny's dolls are hand-me-downs. They are ruled over by a china doll that Danny's not allowed to touch. She stands about two and a half feet tall and sits on a high shelf. Her golden coils of hair bounce on her shoulders, and her blue eyes blink. She wears a navy blue sailor dress with gold trim and little white leather shoes that button up the side.

Down lower on the shelves, within Danny's grasp, is a row of dolls that he is allowed to play with. These are more durable dolls, dolls that are made of plastic. They all have more or less the same face, regardless of age or size. They are bride dolls and Barbie dolls and baby dolls, and though they have no personality, they have a carton full of clothes.

On the floor, sprawling over pillows and window sills, and hanging out of open drawers, are the rag dolls. The rag dolls have been in the family for who knows how many years and they are virtually indestructible, or rather, they are beyond destructible because they are already destroyed. Their faces are blackened with grime and dust. Their woolen hair, once red, brown, black and gold has now gone mostly gray, and their clothes are torn and soiled. Since they have no value, Danny is allowed to take the rag dolls outside, and he can often be seen walking down the sidewalk dragging his red wagon behind him, the rag dolls bumping along and hanging over the sides. From time to time, one will fall out of the wagon, and he'll pick it up and throw it back in, or maybe not see it happen and find it later. Or maybe it will get run over by a passing car or left out in the rain to be discovered later by a neighbor.

There are six rag dolls in the wagon today. The seventh has been left at home, because Danny has hidden her under his bed. In the front of the wagon sit Papa and Mama, side by side, staring backwards and supervising the four kids. The parents are an old Raggedy Ann and Andy pair, once blond and light-skinned but now filmed in gray. The triplets, lying atop one another, are medium-sized brown felt dolls with dark woolly hair and stunned button eyes. They have wide red mouths that sometimes look smug and other times look sad, but you could never actually say they ever smiled. They wear what they have always worn—rags—along with whatever Danny happens to put on them. This morning, one wears a diaper, another a shirt, and another has an arm and two legs through a pink dress. Danny calls them Benda, Betty and Biff. The fourth member of the family

CHAPTER 3: Meeting a Heroine

is a smaller Andy doll with blazing orange hair, and he is dressed in blue overalls. Danny calls him Undee.

Now we come to the doll under Danny's bed. She is a recent acquisition—a big, chocolate-colored felt doll, larger than Mama and Papa. She has short stiff black hair and she wears a white and blue print dress with once-white socks and black patent leather shoes. She's a gift from Danny's Aunt Leah who came over last month with the doll in a huge bag. When she pulled out the doll, almost three quarters Danny's size, Danny was so surprised that he lurched backward, lost his footing, and wailed, watering the carpet like a sprinkler on a lawn.

As they bump along in the wagon, the other dolls are relieved that Danny could not find the big doll today. Last week when Danny put her in the wagon, she caused so much jostling that the dolls lost Emma, the little teddy bear, who was dear to everybody's heart. The family has not finished their grieving, nor have they stopped resenting that big stupid doll for sending Emma over the side.

Danny hasn't named her, and to tell the truth, he didn't spend much time looking for her this morning because he really doesn't know what to do with Leah's gift. For her part, she is happy to hide under the bed, knowing that lack of recognition has its own rewards.

Soon Danny comes home and marches upstairs, his arms loaded with dolls. He throws them down on the bed and leaves, slamming the door behind him. Papa tumbles to the floor, and it is not long before he notices the big doll lying under the bed. He chuckles.

"How's life in the dark?" he asks.

"I think I prefer it," comes the reply.

"Yep, but it can be awful lonely," says Papa with a twinkle in his eye. "Out here, we get loved to death."

They lie in silence for a few minutes and then the big doll says, "I'm sorry about Emma." Papa is suddenly at a loss for words now that he's been reminded. He's still feeling rather bitter about that.

Bang! A door slams and Danny comes running up the stairs with his mother chasing after him. "That's right," she can be heard hollering, "You go to your room and don't you come out again, you brat. I don't want to see your face till dinner time!" *Whack!* A backhand to Danny's butt followed by a new outbreak of screams. What the commotion is all about the dolls can only guess. Probably Danny got into the bathroom again, and started stuffing paper down the hole and flushing, flushing. It's the one thing that will drive his mother wild and bring her charging like a bull from the sitting room.

CHAPTER 3: Meeting a Heroine

The bedroom door flies open and Danny lurches in. Outside, his mother props a chair against the door handle and Danny is a prisoner. Stinging with pain, in tears and flames, he flings himself onto the pile of dolls on the bed. They go flying in all directions as fists and knees and feet pound the bed like hail. The tantrum lasts for several minutes, and, after a couple of short squalls, the storm dies. Danny lies spent on the bed, observing a few moments of silence, and then he goes to fetch his rag dolls. He gathers up the whole family and sits on the floor under the window sill, clutching them to his chest. The tears spring again from his eyes and shower the motley crew. Then he happens to see a little black patent leather shoe gleaming in the dark under the bed. His tears stop, and he reaches forward to drag the doll out into the light.

She slides out from under the bed like a pizza from the oven. Danny stares at the doll. "I hate you," he says. He grabs her by the neck and turns her on himself. "Well, I hate you too," he makes her say. Then he turns her on the others. "I hate all of you. You and you and you." Swinging her like a golf club, he whacks at the other dolls so they go flying around the room.

From that day on, Danny uses the big black doll to boss the others around, just as his mother bosses him around. He calls her Bossy and the dolls grow to hate her even more than they did before. Now when he takes the dolls out in his wagon it is Bossy who decides who will go and who won't. Bossy takes the best seat, and the rest are reduced to fourth class citizens, more at risk than ever now that big Bossy rides in the cart.

Time goes by, and the dolls become alarmed at the increase of violence in their lives. Not that they hoped for hospitality, but Danny's abuse has gone beyond the pale. Papa gets the brunt of it. Danny makes Bossy attack Papa for things he wouldn't dream of doing, like beating his wife and children. It appears that Danny is out to destroy the head of the family, the one who is dearest to the dolls, the only one among them who can make them laugh at the ironies of life.

Then one day, while Danny is dragging his wagon down the sidewalk, a horrible thing happens. The neighbor's dog, a huge unneutered black lab, bolts from the house on the corner and comes loping towards Danny with a maniacal look in his eye. In terror, Danny grabs Papa and hurls him onto the neighbor's lawn to distract the dog. Then he abandons his wagon of dolls and goes running home in fear of his life. Later, his mother comes out and rescues the wagon, but by then Papa is long gone, and the whole cartload of dolls has seen him dismembered by the cruel dog.

After that terrible day, Danny makes things worse by using Bossy to blame the other dolls for throwing Papa to the dog. Again and again he opens the wound of their loss. To say the dolls hate Bossy now is an understatement. Undee, the

CHAPTER 3: Meeting a Heroine

orange-haired boy doll, is ready to wage war on Bossy and he fills the girls' heads full of violent fantasies about doing her in.

"It's all stuff and nonsense," says Mama. "We can't do anything about Bossy. We're all just a bunch of dolls! We're nothing but objects, acted upon by the blind forces of nature."

Benda, Betty and Biff sob, remembering every harrowing moment of Papa's awful torment in the jaws of the dog. Together they go over and over it again, taking apart Papa's taking-apart so many times that their hatred of Bossy grows into a fierce rage.

For her part, Bossy is in a serious dilemma. It isn't her nature to be bossy. It never was. She is a gentle doll. She had the lovely name of Linda before she entered this hellish place. Leah treated her doll as a person in her own right, so Linda's gentle nature naturally flowed out. They were true friends when Leah was a child, but then she grew up and forgot who Linda was.

How can she tell the others that it isn't in her nature to be bossy? They don't believe in their own natures, much less hers. Dolls, as Mama is constantly reminding them, are made up only of what children imagine them to be, and nothing more. There is no chance in the world that they will believe Linda is anything but bossy, especially not with Danny picking her up every moment he can find and asserting her against them.

Inside, Linda is mourning Papa too. He only spoke to her two or three times, but those moments were precious to her. Now she can no longer tolerate being used as an instrument of abuse. She must find a way to assert herself. Stop the abuse. Get out of the loop. But how?

For some time, she struggles with the question. Then an idea begins to dawn. Maybe she can't control Danny's thoughts, but can she control her own? What if she blocked Danny's thoughts from coming into her head? If she could do that somehow, then at least she might win a little room to be herself. That, she concludes, is the most she can hope for.

The next day, when Danny goes to pick Bossy up and make her tell the others what a mess they made overnight, he suddenly can't remember what it is he wants to say. "Stupid doll," he says. Feeling stupid himself, he kicks her across the room. He throws himself on the bed and pouts, glaring at the doll. He decides that he doesn't like her, not at all. He won't play with her anymore. She's a stupid doll.

Days go by and he avoids having anything to do with Bossy. As a result, he becomes more frustrated and lonely than ever. He decides that all his rag dolls are stupid and he doesn't want to play with any of them anymore. He takes a few of

CHAPTER 3: Meeting a Heroine

the plastic dolls off the shelf, and changes their clothes for a while but his heart isn't in it.

For the first time since as long as they can remember, the rag dolls are unwanted, liberated from Danny's love. They're free to enjoy the sun on the sill, the shade under the bed. Amongst themselves, they take another look at Bossy. What is this glorious freedom that she has won for them all? What has she done to Danny? Why does Danny suddenly think his rag dolls are stupid? Why is he not able to make Bossy boss them anymore?

Eventually, Undee gathers the nerve to ask Bossy, "Hey, what are you up to?" Bossy doesn't say anything, which causes them to speculate. The girls begin to consider the possibility that dolls may have power after all. Can a doll manipulate the human mind? They wonder. Surely not, we're just objects. Aren't we? Mama assures them they are, and that Danny is simply bored. The peace will pass. But the more Benda, Betty, Biff and Undee watch Bossy, the more convinced they become that she is influencing Danny with her thoughts. Somehow.

Then one day, Danny can stand it no longer. He comes in his room, grabs Bossy and flings himself on the bed with her. He hugs her to his chest because he really, really did miss her. Then he goes to turn her on the other dolls on the floor, but the thing that has been happening happens again. His thoughts get blocked, and he stammers. For just one second, he forgets to get angry because his love and his hate get crisscrossed, and in that moment, Bossy turns to him and says, "I don't hate you at all, Danny."

Danny is absolutely flabbergasted; frightened, even. Though he heard his own voice say it, it wasn't his own thought. He throws her down and runs out of the room to fetch his mother, who comes in, takes the doll away and puts her on a high shelf in her room. But Danny can't stay away. Back and forth, up and down the hall he goes, all afternoon until he can stand it no more. He goes to his mother's room, climbs on a chair and takes the doll down. He carries her back to his room and clambers up on the bed, clinging to her like a chimp mother to her baby.

Linda, knowing that he has been frightened, is careful not to shock him again. Instead, she lets her nature out slowly, asking him questions that feel to him more like his own thoughts, such as, "How was your day? How are you doing?" and he starts to confide in her as if she were a friend and not a doll.

Meanwhile, the dolls are saying, "Hey, would you look at that? Look at what Bossy's got going up there with Danny!" Their hatred for Bossy begins to transform into admiration. They whisper amongst themselves, swapping legends about how Bossy came to liberate them, and, as time goes by, they make Bossy into a heroine they now call "the Boss."

Yet "the Boss" doesn't respond to their adulation any more than she did to their hatred. The dolls get to thinking, "Hey, what about us? The Boss is up there all the time with Danny, and she's not representing the rest of us. She's a doll after all. She should remember her roots. She should be doing something for us." So when Danny is out of the room, the dolls, led by Undee, say, "Look, you're the Boss, you've got a voice now, you can speak for all of us. Tell Danny to show us some respect. Tell Danny that he should put us on the shelf and clean us up and change our clothes like he does with the plastic dolls." And so on.

Linda doesn't know what to do about the other dolls' requests, and they won't stop bothering her about it. She can't fill Danny's head with all that stuff. She doesn't have the power, and even if she did, she wouldn't like to manipulate Danny any more than she would like to be manipulated. It's up to Danny to think his own thoughts, she decides. Then one day while she's on the bed and the rag dolls are hounding her from around the room, she gets mad at the whole pack of them and says, "Look, stop bossing me around!"

Does that ever stop them short! The whole rag doll family reels in astonishment. How dare she turn on her own kind and accuse them of being bossy! For weeks they simmer and seethe, and then they return to calling her Bossy and hating her. Well, that's okay, she's used to that. Danny treats her kindly, and that's his choice, and the dolls resent her and that's their choice. Danny is careful and gentle with her. He won't take her in the wagon with all the other dolls in case something happens to her. As for the rest of the dolls, he treats them more or less like he's always treated them, which is to say, not very well. But anyway, there's enough room in the wagon now. Nobody ever falls out.

CHAPTER 3: Meeting a Heroine

CHAPTER 3: Meeting a Heroine

"Danny was so surprised that he lurched backward, lost his footing and wailed, watering the carpet like a sprinkler on a lawn."

Like Danny, I'm knocked off my feet by this great big doll. The prisoner meets the liberated woman. She's too big for me. She's gonna make me change, she's gonna bust up my security, and I feel like wailing and running away, just like Danny did.

As I was reading the story though, I got to thinking, Wow, maybe this gal is gonna be able to handle Cadwell. Maybe she'll turn things around in here. (And in particular, maybe she'll protect me, carve out some sort of niche for me.) But that's not how the story ends. The big Linda doll doesn't liberate the others. They stay exactly where they started off: in the wagon. The only one she liberates is herself. Is that heroic?

I guess I have some hidden expectation that the people above should defend the people below in this period of turmoil. Or at least toss us a life jacket if they're gonna throw us off the boat. Maybe I'm being unrealistic. Managers are driven by economic forces just like the rest of us. Some are being used to whack us around, and others are hiding their true natures out of fear. Then there are those who may be liberated but they don't see freeing us as part of their responsibility. So whose responsibility is it to free us? OURS? Maybe, but dammit, I resent the indifference. The demeaning. And the assumption that we're supposed to have a clue how to be free.

CHAPTER 4

Call to Adventure

CHAPTER 4: Call to Adventure

A Seeker's Journal

February 20

What a bleak day. It started this morning when I woke up at about 6 a.m. to the sound of the dog next door howling like he'd just lost his best friend. The sun rose an hour or two later, faint-hearted, like it didn't want to. I thought, this is what depression is, I want to hide under the covers and never get up. Life has definitely lost its savor. I really don't know what I live for. I am a droid watching myself get replaced by someone who is free. I don't have much life outside of work. I came here for the job. My folks live out west, along with my closest friends. I didn't choose to live here, it just happened. In fact, when I think about it, I didn't choose much in my life. I've just sort of bumped around from one thing to the next, doing what seemed like the obvious, sensible thing to do at the time. I feel so average. The only thing that I'm actually good at is doodling. I am an excellent doodler.

Anyway, waking up this morning was the high point of the day. It descended to such a low that I might have perished if Caroline hadn't come along to scrape me off the pavement.

In a nutshell, here's what happened. Over the last few months, we've been hit by a huge wave of layoffs. Last week the "survivors" were called to an early morning meeting in which we were told that management would not be laying anybody else off for some time. So I come in this morning and guess what's sitting on my desk? A letter from the Human Resources department informing A. Seeker that his job has become "redundant due to necessary measures to reengineer the media communications department." I was floored. What happened? Did this letter get lost? Did it bump around a dozen departments before it found its way to me? I can imagine people looking at the envelope asking, "Who is A. Seeker?" Thinking it's some kind of a joke.

I had a whole bunch of appointments to line up and then we had a video shoot this afternoon. I went through the whole day like a dead man, drained of all sensation. Around 4 o'clock I realized that I wasn't even in my body. I was just watching from the sidelines, watching how pathetic it all was, how inane and meaningless most human activity is.

At 5, Caroline said, "Let me buy you a drink." I guess she had heard what happened. We took the stairwell to the EXIT. As we came downstairs, we looked out the window and saw this amazing rainbow. Brilliant colors against the dark sky—the boldest and most awesome rainbow I have ever seen. We stood there staring at it together and then we proceeded down the steps in silence, like we had both seen a vision.

CHAPTER 4: Call to Adventure

We drove her car to a jazz bar-restaurant she likes; a happy place, with comfortable booths and colorful artwork hanging everywhere. I drank scotch on the rocks. I showed her the letter and she agreed it was pretty brutal. Then she asked me, "What are you gonna do now?"

I shrugged. "I don't know. What can I do?"

"Produce videos, for starters. Go out on your own, start your own company. I'd hire you."

"I dunno."

She smiled, leaned across the table and whispered, "You're free, A. Seeker. Return to the wild."

CHAPTER 4: Call to Adventure

FROM THE DESK OF A. SEEKER

"The Permanent Cat" was told at a workshop I went to called "How to Become Self-Employed." We were asked to share an example of when we initiated some venture or project in the past. My mind went blank. I kept thinking, "I'm not made of the right stuff for this." Everybody else had something to offer. I sat there like a rock. A giant, unmovable boulder. Anyway, I liked the story. It assured me there are other "cats" out there who feel the same way as I do.

CHAPTER 4: Call to Adventure

The Permanent Cat

There was once a cat by the name of Mr. Tibbs. A very fine cat, indeed. A sleek and gray Siamese. Mr. Tibbs had been a loyal house cat all his life, and was proud of his long service as a mouser.

So you can imagine his surprise when his mistress put him out on the street one day. "I'm sorry, Mr. Tibbs," she said, "but there isn't a mouse in the house anymore, so we haven't a need for you. Thank you for your long service, dear, you've been very sweet." She gave him a recommendation, rolled it into his collar and shut the door.

Poor Mr. Tibbs! He felt downright betrayed. He had been in that house for seven years! All the same, he reminded himself, he was a fine cat, a Siamese, and a very good mouser, indeed. Surely there ought to be others with mice who were interested in a permanent cat. So he went to the house down the street.

He meowed. An old man opened the door. He had white hair and kindly eyes. "Hello," purred Mr. Tibbs. "My name is Mr. Tibbs. I am 7 years old, and I am looking for a permanent home. I am a fine mouser. I am loyal and fully domesticated. In short, I am a permanent cat." He cocked his head to one side, looking very proud.

"I'm sorry," said the old man. "I can't take a permanent cat."

"Don't you have mice?" asked Mr. Tibbs.

"Well, yes, I've got mice, and I'd like to be rid of them too, but like I said, I can't take a permanent cat."

The old man shut the door. Mr. Tibbs walked down the alleyway, confused. He tried another door, and then another. It was the same story. Lots of mice, but no one would take a permanent cat.

Late in the day, while he was pawing through some trash trying to scare up dinner, along came an alley cat. She bounded through the litter, causing every living thing to jump and run. There was dinner all around her. Mr. Tibbs crouched and growled. Who did she think she was, making such a commotion? You would think she had the world by the tail.

She leaped on top of the garbage can above Mr. Tibb's head. "Well, well, what do we have here?" she purred. "A fine gentleman."

"A permanent cat," said Mr. Tibbs.

She laughed and jumped off the lid of the can. "A permanent cat? Well, I suppose I'm a permanent cat too. Permanently independent." She began to saunter off.

47

"Wait a minute," said Mr. Tibbs following her. "Don't you work? Don't you need strokes like the rest of us?"

"Oh, I need strokes," she said. "I am currently employed by Mr. Beetleham, down on 53rd. But I don't suppose he's going to have mice forever."

"Then what will you do?"

"I'll go someplace else."

"Whatever happened to the principle of loyalty?" said Mr. Tibbs, sulking.

The alley cat stopped. She surveyed him. She sidled by him. She walked around him. "What's your name?" she purred.

"Mr. Tibbs," he said, gathering himself up.

"Well, Mr. Tibbs. You're a fine cat, I can see that. But if you want to survive you're going to have to take a little walk on the wild side. Let go of all that permanent stuff. Follow me. I'll show you how to make the transition."

So Mr. Tibbs followed the alley cat. After several weeks, he was ready to seek employment once again, and he returned to the old man's house. He had liked the look of that sofa in the living room.

He meowed at the door and the old man opened it. "Hello," purred Mr. Tibbs. "My name is Mr. Tibbs. I understand you have a problem with mice."

"I do indeed," said the old man.

"I see. And do you have any other needs in a cat?"

"Well, I could do with a little companionship. But I'm old, you know. I don't want to worry about a cat if I have to move on."

"Well, sir," said Mr. Tibbs, "I have been a domestic cat for seven years, so I make an excellent companion, and I have the references to prove it. I am also a trained mouser. And because I am completely independent, I will have no trouble surviving if you have to put me back out on the street. I will also return to the street if I am unhappy in your home."

"Oh, you dear cat," said the old man. "I will do my utmost to give you the best home I can." He lifted him up, and took him inside.

So Mr. Tibbs got a special place on the sofa, his favorite food and lots of strokes. He loved the old man, and his love was permanent—though he never forgot, he wasn't a permanent cat.

CHAPTER 4: Call to Adventure

CHAPTER 4: Call to Adventure

"Whatever happened to the principle of loyalty?" said Mr. Tibbs, sulking.

Up until now, loyalty has been my main principle. I am much more like the permanent cat than the alley cat. I'm used to domesticity. I've grown accustomed to my cage. Suddenly the gate is flung open and Caroline says, "You're free!" and all I can do is panic and think, No! Why the hell did they open the door? Shut the door! What am I going to do out there?

I've spent my whole life becoming domesticated: I'm house-broken. Broken. I once saw an elephant being broken. A baby Indian elephant. They tied his four legs to four trees and they harassed him, whipped him, humiliated him. He roared and fought but eventually he fell to his knees. The scene made me weep. When it was over, he had become a patient, obedient, compliant elephant. Like all the rest of us. Without any equipment for the wild.

The good news is they didn't completely domesticate me, I stood up to Cadwell. I'm proud of that. Maybe there's hope for me yet ....

CHAPTER 5

Finding the Orphan

A Seeker's Journal

March 27

I've been at home for three weeks. I don't know where the days go, they just sift between my fingers like sand. I keep thinking, It's not sand, it's gold. You're wasting the gold. The first week, I got up every day, went out for a fast walk, went by the corner store and got a paper. I stayed on a schedule, determined to find a job. Then I started to get up later and I stopped going outside. Now, like today, like right now, I'm just lying in bed at some indeterminate time of day. Noticing that I haven't bought new sheets for about ten years. Noticing that this room, this apartment, bears all the markings of neglect, of belonging to someone who doesn't spend much time at home. Home should be where the heart is. My heart's been in my work. No, that's a lie. My heart's been nowhere. It's been hiding out. Glad for the reprieve. Glad not to be broken.

I have this underlying churning anxiety that keeps me up at night and makes me depressed during the day. The phone hardly ever rings, I feel like my life is over. The other day I went wandering downtown and I stood on the corner trying to decide if I was going to go into the art gallery. Part of me really wanted to go in, the other part felt like it was going to be sick. I couldn't make a decision. In the end, I went home.

My life has gone completely out of focus. There's nothing in the foreground. I've been shot into the background. I don't know what's important anymore. My life bears no outstanding features. It's all one big blur.

April 1

Here's a little something for April Fools ... I got a letter today from the HR folks at Commercial Life. They're offering me a contract position in internal communications. It goes till August. The position involves writing internal communications documents, with a chance of getting involved in training, so "there is a possibility that the position may be a potential opportunity for growth." I can just see that scared communications writer carefully putting in the qualifiers to cover everyone's butt. Wouldn't wanna make any false promises or nothin'.

My initial reaction was relief. Now I know where I can earn some income. I've got enough stashed away to get me through a couple of months, maybe a few more if I sell my car ... but then I'll be desperate.

I haven't seen Caroline for a few weeks. Maybe she'll have some insight into the job.

CHAPTER 5: Finding the Orphan

April 3

Caroline and I went back to that bar-restaurant we went to the day I was laid off. I really like the place. It combines three of my favorite things in one room: food, alcohol and art. I'm attracted to the paintings, they're so bold ... primary colors against dark backgrounds, like that rainbow we saw out the window of the stairwell. They're acrylics, done in a primitive, almost childlike style. Naive and adept at the same time. Reminiscent of Chagall. Rich colors, big scenes, highly illustrative, seen from weird angles. There's a tension to them—sharp dark edges, ominous shadows and danger zones.

I asked Caroline, "Do you know this guy?" She said he's the cousin of the manager. He's got a lot of money and sometimes comes into the restaurant. "I've never seen him, but I wouldn't mind. He's supposed to be really good looking. And rich. They call him 'the Prince.'" She twirled the celery in her Caesar. I felt a wave of jealousy.

The conversation fell into a hole of silence. I tried to save it by telling her about the job offer. I made an effort to sound excited about it, like, "You know, I mean I could maybe, possibly, potentially get into training, that would be pretty cool.

She stifled a yawn. Her disinterest was hurtful. Downright offensive.

Then she said, "I found some of your storyboards the other day."

"Oh yeah?"

"Storyboards that you have obviously never produced."

I thought I had cleaned out my stuff from the office ... doodles, the mindless fantasies of an involuntary celibate. Oh crap.

"I didn't know you could draw like that. I actually read one of the boards. Not only did I read it, I got involved in it. That one about the mountain that becomes a dragon ... wow."

I confessed to Caroline that I've been known to doodle to pass the time. Then, as she was crunching her celery, I went further. I said I had this crazy dream to illustrate children's books. It really is a crazy dream. I don't know why it's so crazy. But it is.

"You say you doodle," said Caroline, moving the drink away and leaning forward so close I caught the scent of her. "What does that mean? What is doodling exactly?"

"Well, drawing, I guess, but I'm not really paying attention. It happens more or less unconsciously."

She looked at me like I was really thick. "I know what doodling is, Albert. Why don't you call it drawing? Why are you trivializing your gift?"

CHAPTER 5: Finding the Orphan

"I call it doodling because it is, by definition, a waste of time. You can't make a living doodling."

Caroline looked like she had been hit in the face. She said, "Are you going to measure everything you love for the rest of your life on the basis of whether or not it will make you a living? What about something that needs you to make IT living? Why would you orphan your own gift?"

I couldn't believe she said "orphan." I had just read a story about an orphan, and at that moment, all I could see in front of me was his pale, white face.

CHAPTER 5: Finding the Orphan

FROM THE DESK OF A. SEEKER

I had read "The Orphan" in a magazine that was lying on the counter at The Café Olé. I went back for it but I couldn't find the magazine, so I had to go to the reference library to find it.

CHAPTER 5: Finding the Orphan

The Orphan

Hannah never gave birth, but she had a child. A little one who sat at the gates between heaven and earth, waiting to come in. Waiting and waiting like he would wait forever. She couldn't conceive him but she knew he was there. She could feel him waiting. She was tormented by the image of that child sitting there. It was with her day and night. What had she done, she wondered, to be given a child but not be given the key to open the gates and bring him into the world?

She went through years of anguish, trying to get pregnant; years of being poked and prodded, of seeking without solutions, only to find herself back at the gates, grieving and shaking the bars. You can't keep something like that up forever. Finally, nearing 40, she couldn't do it anymore. She had to accept the impossibility of ever conceiving. She had to move on.

She went into her heart and she sat down at the gate with the child of her dreams. "I can't seem to open the gates for you, little one," she said. "You know I've tried every way possible. Maybe you're not meant to come in." She couldn't see him behind the gate, but she could feel him nestling up to her, listening from behind the bars. She could feel the warmth of his little body, a rustle of wings. "I think you belong in heaven, and I belong here," she said. "You can't keep waiting for me. You need to go on about your business … but if you must come to earth, find another gate because, my little one, I can't open this one for you." Then she said the hardest thing of all: "I have to go now, and I won't be back. Maybe I'll catch up with you in heaven. Good-bye little one. Good-bye."

The child didn't go away. He stayed there at the gates, trying to peer through the bars to see back into her life.

She stopped thinking about him and went on with her work. She wrote stories for children, and, perhaps because she was no longer at war inside, her stories came thick and fast.

One rainy night, Hannah and her husband John got off a bus, crossed the street and headed quickly to the subway, huddled together under a shared umbrella. They passed a park where a little boy sat alone on a bench under the lamplight. He wore a ragged maroon sweater and frayed beige pants. His thin blond hair fell about his shoulders, streaming rain. He had round blue eyes that widened when he looked up, and a sweet little mouth, the color of wine. She stopped. "Who is that little boy?" she asked John.

"Just a street kid," he said. "Let's go."

But she couldn't go farther. She turned back to the boy on the bench.

CHAPTER 5: Finding the Orphan

She sat down beside him. "What are you doing here?" she asked gently. "Shouldn't you be home by now?" He couldn't be more than seven or eight years old.

His cheeks flushed a little, and he smiled shyly, showing a row of tender teeth. She noticed his lashes were long and darker than his hair, but his face was terribly thin.

"You don't belong here, little lamb," she said. He said nothing. Instead, he passed her his white hand, as if he were prepared to go wherever she wished.

She looked at John with surprise.

"Well, let's go get something to eat. It looks as if you could use it," he said.

So they went to a restaurant on the corner of Stewart and Main. They took a booth and when the waitress came, they ordered all kinds of food to please the boy, who didn't seem to be the least bit interested in what they ordered or how yummy they made it all sound. He squinted in the light of the restaurant and rubbed his eyes as if he had never been exposed to the light.

Hannah kept trying to figure out where she had seen this boy, why he was so familiar. Maybe on TV, maybe they had done a special on street kids or something. But her feeling of recognition was much stronger than a faded television image. She couldn't stop staring at him, sitting there shivering and rubbing his eyes as if he'd just woken up.

All of a sudden she was seized with the urge to get him to a place of safety. They couldn't just feed him and return him to the streets. She wrenched herself away from the table, and called Children's Aid.

She told the man on the other end that she had found a boy in the park. She gave him a detailed description, adding that the boy didn't appear to be able to speak. After sitting on hold several times, a woman came on the line who said she would send a social worker.

She returned to the table where her husband sat with the boy. The food had arrived—burgers, salad, chicken fingers, onion rings—but it was all pushed to one side. Neither her husband nor the boy were eating. John gazed at a space on the table, his gray-bearded face twisted into an odd mixture of wonder and apprehension.

It seemed the boy had become interested in the menu, in the feel of its smooth laminated surface. He swept his thin white hand over the page and flipped it up, sending a colorful ghost of the paper into the air. The paper ghost floated for a moment, and then dissolved. He did this over and over again, making the paper fly in different colors: green, pink, purple, blue, red and orange. They sat under the floating, falling leaves like children under a magical tree.

CHAPTER 5: Finding the Orphan

"He's not a child," Hannah whispered. "He's an angel. Oh my God, he's an angel."

The boy looked at her through the rainbow leaves and let out a musical little laugh, as if he had just heard his name.

Then the social worker came. She was a large, officious woman who wore heavy black shoes and white socks. She presented her card. She had papers that needed to be filled out. The food was sent away. The boy put his hands on his lap and lowered his head. He did not smile again, nor make any more colorful paper fly. The social worker assessed him over her bifocals and said he probably lived at the orphanage, though she had never seen him before. He gave no answer to her questions. She suspected that he was autistic. Finally, she took his hand and led him away. Hannah insisted on going with him, at least to the car.

Outside, the rain had turned to snow and it sleeted down at a sharp angle. They trod carefully through the streets, pulling their coats tightly around them, except for the boy, ran crisply alongside the social worker to keep up with her steps.

They came to a van and the social worker yanked open the doors at the back with brute strength. Patting the boy on the bum, she hurried him up the steps and onto a bench in the van. He sat there, teeth chattering. Hannah wanted to take him home right there and then but she knew she couldn't, not then. She would find a way. Tomorrow. It was the only thing that comforted her when they shut the door on his intense little white face.

The next day, Hannah called the Children's Aid to inquire about the boy, but nobody knew who she was talking about. She went down to the office that afternoon, demanding to see him. She gave the woman at the desk the social worker's card, but the clerk said no one worked there with that name, nor did they recognize the worker's description. She also said that Children's Aid doesn't pick up children in vans and they never take them to orphanages. "In this country, children are given foster homes," she declared in a rather off-putting way. Hannah went home, feeling deserted and confused. It took her months to pick up the pieces, but in time she resolved that he wasn't an orphan. Never was, never would be.

Now, if you ask Hannah, "Do you have any children?" she will reply: "Oh yes, I have a child, but he prefers to stay in heaven." That's all, and you'll wonder what the heck she's talking about. But then, if you ask her how her writing is going, she might go to her desk and flip through some pages, looking for something she feels like reading. And while you're sitting there watching her, you find yourself getting kind of excited, because you know you are about to be sailed off to a magical place ... a garden in childhood ... where you played till the end of the day ... till the stars came out in the china-blue sky ... and the light went gold

CHAPTER 5: Finding the Orphan

and the moon rose ... and you pretended you were in heaven so you would never have to come home.

CHAPTER 5: Finding the Orphan

CHAPTER 5: Finding the Orphan

"They shut the door on his intense little white face."

Hannah might have found a way to keep her connection with that orphan, but I got stuck at the place where he went away. The story saddened me when I first read it and does even more so now.

It was my Dad who said, "You can't make a living doodling." He was a gym teacher, my Dad. He would praise my drawings but at the same time, he would mock me for the time I spent "doodling." "You're just goofing off, Albert," he would say. "Why don't you go out and do something productive?"

I dawdled, I doodled, I daydreamed, I did all the things that a boy likes to do but is told he shouldn't. This subterranean anxiety that is with me all the time comes from way back. It's guilt; the feeling that I have no business enjoying one moment of life, that I ought to be putting my nose to the grindstone, and grinding till I can't smell the roses anymore and there's nothing in my head but facts and a cold, hard business sense.

My parents were embarrassed that their only son wanted to be an artist, and was coming up dumb. My grades were not good and I didn't even like sports. They put pressure on me in elementary school; tried praise and punishment, but nothing worked. They didn't have another son or daughter to shift the pressure to because my older sister Alison has a mental disability. I think they felt that their kids would never amount to anything.

So yeah, they were pretty happy with me when I went back to high school to pick up credits and then enrolled in college. They were thrilled when I went out and got a job working as a camera man for a cable television station. When I started working in insurance they couldn't keep from boasting to their friends: "Albert's a video producer for Commercial Life." I didn't turn out so bad after all.

I haven't told them that I got laid off. I stare at this letter here and I am so tempted to accept because then I don't have to face my parents' disappointment. Really, when you get right down to it, it's their disapproval that stands between me and doing something totally different with my life. I can feel their fear that I'm going to return to that dumb, goof-off kid they are pretty convinced I am, deep down.

But that orphan boy is here again. I let him go once, and here he is again. I'd like to rationalize that I'll see him again tomorrow, but my gut says, "If you don't chase after that van right now, he's going to fade into the background and be lost to you forever."

CHAPTER 6

Leap to Freedom

CHAPTER 6: Leap to Freedom

A Seeker's Journal

April 12

Am I nuts? I must be nuts. I've done it. I wrote and turned the offer down. Oh God, I am nuts.

I went for a walk. A very brisk walk down by the lakeshore. The wind was cold, but not so cutting as it was a few weeks ago. Spring is almost here. You can feel the wind softening. The gusts are becoming more gentle, like angels flapping their wings, moving you along. I felt like running, like I could fly. If I just held my breath and thought "light," I would take off.

I am so happy. I don't know where I get off being so happy. I've got two or three months left of my savings and I haven't gone down to the unemployment office. I'm full of hope, irrational hope that everything is going to be all right.

What do I do now? Hell if I know. But it is thrilling to make a decision based on a gut instinct rather than some outer perception of what I should do. I keep thinking about that restaurant that Caroline took me to. What was it called? Silvano's. I used to wait tables before I went to college. I worked in several pretty upscale restaurants. I can wait tables with my eyes closed. I could work at night and give myself some time—see if I can tease something out of my depths and become someone different than who I am now.

The scared, confused part of me says, "This is nuts, you're nuts, you've been listening to a crazy woman and you're probably just flying on lust," and yeah, that's all true. But I'm flying. Flying high.

CHAPTER 6: Leap to Freedom

FROM THE DESK OF A. SEEKER

After I turned the job offer down, Carolina and I went by subway to pick Christopher up from school. He dumped his pack on the seat and a book fell out, opening to this story, "The Butterflower." You might say the story landed at my feet.

CHAPTER 6: Leap to Freedom

The Butterflower

One day, high on a mountain, in an alpine meadow, a butterflower appeared. Her yellow petals fluttered in the breeze with such a soft, buttery motion that the Wind fell in love. He couldn't get enough of waving the butterflower to and fro, and so he scattered her pollen all over the earth.

Now the Wind was able to visit her everywhere, and the earth was covered in one rolling sea of butter. Scrumptious. But it wasn't enough for the Wind to visit her everywhere and run his breezes through her hair. He wanted to lift her up, to fly her over all the world, to see her reflected in all the colors of the sun.

"Come," said the Wind to the butterflower, "Join me in the sky. Release yourself from your stalk and trade! Fly!"

"No, no!" cried the butterflower. "I have my roots to think about. If you take me, I will die!"

The Wind blew a little harder, easing her from her roots. "I would never let you die," he whispered. "Who could love you more than I?"

Now, the butterflower was attracted to the Wind, and she had been for a long time. Deep down, she had to admit that even one second in flight with the Wind would be better than all the moments she had spent rooted to the ground.

So, one day, she let the Wind detach her from her stalk. Up and up she flew. She could not see, she could only feel the wonderful sensation of the Wind lifting her into the air. So gentle and caressing was he that she began to relax and trust. Antennae grew from her head, and when her eyes appeared, the whole world opened up below her, like one huge, unfolding flower.

"Look at me!" she shouted to the other flowers. "I can fly! Let the Wind take you. You'll flower even better in the sky!" Many heard her call and let go of their stalks, but many more stayed behind.

To this day, the butterfly remains the flower of the Wind. Most of the flowers disdain her in her caterpillar stage, and forget her when she's wrapped in her cocoon. But when the Wind comes to wake her from her sleep, they are all amazed. And many is the flower that waits, hoping the Wind will fall in love again!

CHAPTER 6: Leap to Freedom

CHAPTER 6: Leap to Freedom

"I would never let you die, who could love you more than I?"

The wind is real. This tremendous sense of support and confidence buoys me up. I've decided to trust it. You know that saying, "The angels have gone before you and all the lights are green"? That's the way it feels. I'm having really good dreams, spectacular, brightly colored dreams, like my life has gone from black and white to Technicolor overnight.

I've been sitting in my apartment for days, staring out the window, just staring. Somehow I needed to get it out of my system, all the staring out the window I couldn't do as a kid. Spending time in the background is like breathing in a tonic I've needed like air.

On the outside, nothing's going on. My life has come to a standstill. I should be feeling panic, humiliation, depression, despair. That would be the scripted response. But it's not my choice. I'm starting to write my own lines. I'm listening to what's going on inside, waiting for the right direction to arise.

I don't know where I get the trust. I just have it. My head is whirring around, still running the same program, "Are you nuts? Are you nuts?" I'm trying to quiet it down. It's a lot of work, but hey, what else have I got to do?

CHAPTER 7

The Wild Side

CHAPTER 7: The Wild Side

A Seeker's Journal

April 24

Yesterday, I woke up clear-headed. After several weeks of floating around, unfocused, I knew what to do. I called the manager of Silvano's and told him I was an enthusiastic customer with a background as a waiter and a desire to come and work for him.

He said my timing was good. He's expecting to lose one of his waiters in the next few weeks. We arranged a time to meet. All afternoon, I felt mixed up inside, a stew of feelings coming to a boil. I hardly slept last night and when I did I had nightmares. At one point I remember being outside the Earth. I felt this weird, crawling sensation of coming into human skin, reverting from a higher form of me to a primitive ape. I woke upset, confused, needing to know why I had come here, what was the point. I couldn't figure it out.

I have serious misgivings about going back into the restaurant business. I honestly don't know if I have the self-control to handle it. When I was a waiter ten years ago, I got caught in a strong undertow of party life. I did a few too many drugs and became irritable, sarcastic ... even cruel. After my girlfriend moved out, I sank to a place lower than I ever imagined I could go.

I swore I would never go back to the past. Yet here I am, going into old waters, waters that I have to admit feel like home. From the moment I first walked into Silvano's, I got caught up in the atmosphere of artistic people laughing, sharing ideas, telling stories in the candlelight. It stirs up in me a longing that's powerful and magnetic, like the pull of the moon. But I have to say I'm scared that if I let myself down into that water again I won't be able to pull out.

April 28

The manager is Tony Silvano, a portly older guy with a sort of Tibetan monkish feel about him. When he smiles, his whole face creases. He said he could see me fitting in.

CHAPTER 7: The Wild Side

FROM THE DESK OF A. SEEKER

"Seafood Special" resurfaced when I was going through a box of old stories I had collected back in college. The whole waitering thing had got me wanting to clear out some old stuff. I had forgotten that the story involved food and restaurants. But even closer to home, it dealt with reclaiming the wild. (I told my friend Hank I was afraid this job would bring out certain uncivilized aspects of my nature, to which he replied: "Al, you're gonna be a waiter, how weird can you make THAT?")

CHAPTER 7: The Wild Side

Seafood Special

They had been married for fifteen years. They lived in a houseboat, moored in the sleepy little harbor of a small town. They had known one another since school days. Both had been short, round and nameless as far as the other kids were concerned, and they made a bond in fourth grade that would last for life. They had a small wedding with a small cake, and they were given small gifts, like scalloped soap and little coral guest towels with the words HIS and HERS embroidered in white. He had a rather wide mouth, large hands and feet, and thinning auburn hair. He worked as a cook in a seaside restaurant, and seafood was his specialty. She was slightly taller than him, just passing five feet, with only slightly more hope for a svelte physique. She had shoulder length brown hair, fair skin with a dash of pepper on her nose, and small hands that waved and clenched whenever she got excited. Unfortunately she had a rather nervous temperament, and her worry was something you noticed about her immediately, zipping to and fro around her head like some erratic, orbiting moon.

After they married and settled into the boathouse, after she finished finding just the right furniture to match her knickknacks, after the anguish of giving up her crystal because it couldn't survive the storm swells, she turned to her appearance. Now in the middle of her life, she had rounded into a shape that resembled a firm MacIntosh apple. She was not at all pleased with her round, firm look. After ten years of flipping through fashion magazines, she had not yet seen one person whose form even remotely resembled her own. She began to smoke and diet, her heart set on becoming more "chic." She refused her husband's cooking, which hurt his feelings but he didn't say so. He just kept telling her that she was his "Squishy" and her kind of beauty couldn't be matched anywhere. Once she started the dieting, he lost the privilege of looking at her from across the table on Sunday nights during those rocky candlelight dinners he had loved so much. Eating together had been eliminated as one of the two rituals that joined them, and as a result the other one suffered too.

One day, her husband came home with scuba gear and a trainer. They went out through the living room and onto the deck. They sat on the platform with their feet in the water while the trainer talked. Then they both got geared up and disappeared under the water. After about half an hour, they surfaced. The trainer pulled himself up on the platform. He looked discombobulated. He tripped over his flippers as he removed his gear, and he listed to one side instead of standing straight up, which made her worry, gazing on from the living room, that the trainer might have suffered some sort of head injury. Her husband, on the other hand, had no trouble getting out of the water. He tossed his flippers onto the deck and easily slid off his tank.

CHAPTER 7: The Wild Side

"Boy, can you swim," the trainer said.

In the weeks that followed, her husband purchased his own scuba gear, finished his training, and got his certification. After that, every day when he came home from work, he went straight into the water. Several months later the trainer returned to check his student's progress, and after they emerged from the water, all he could say was, "I've never seen anything like it."

Not long after, the trainer came back to the house with an underwater television crew and they filmed her husband swimming. The news report aired the next night. The couple sat on the sofa in the living room, aglow in the sea-green light of the TV. He smiled a wide smile, while she sat bug-eyed and aghast, staring at the man in the film, her husband, who was swimming ... well, not swimming actually, but *squirting* through the water like a frog! It seemed that his legs had grown longer and his feet had widened and the bones had disappeared, making them flap like flippers, and with his big wide smile and his goggles, well, she was shaking with horror when the news clip ended.

"It's just the camera and water effects," he said.

"But why do you swim like that?" she wailed, her hands flapping in front of her. "Why do you swim like a frog? Why don't you swim like everyone else?"

"It wouldn't feel natural," he said. "Besides, I can't get up the speed." And well, he had something there. He could squirt from one place to another faster than the eye could see.

After that, news crews came from other cities, and then even from abroad. People were always milling around on the deck amid wet suits and tanks, gawking down into the sea or descending into the depths of her watery backyard. It was only a matter of time before the movie offers came. Her husband almost never came out of the water now. He had long since quit his job, and an agent from the big city had taken him on. Now he only came up to change his tank, which he seemed to need to do less and less often (and God knows he never needed flippers).

Her horror grew. At first it was distracted by the reporters' interest in her. She gave them a couple of interviews, proud of her new, slightly more svelte physique, until she saw herself on TV. She hardly recognized the pasty, teary-eyed creature before her, who had what appeared to be a terrible case of blackheads spread over her nose. That was the end of her affair with the camera.

Meanwhile, her husband just kept on swimming. He stayed in the water until well after midnight, especially when there was a moon. The agent assured her that when the movie offers started coming, he would have to come up for air, and anyway, the money would entice him back to land. But when the big break did

CHAPTER 7: The Wild Side

come, he refused to leave the water, saying it wouldn't be natural to go and swim anywhere else. This was his home. By that time he had done so much swimming that he had lost the hair on his chest and his legs. The top of his head had gone bald, and all his roundness seemed to have gathered itself in the region of his belly, which was round and firm as a basketball.

"You never eat. What do you eat?" she asked him nervously one morning when he slid into the water.

"Seafood," he said with a wide smile. And he was gone.

One morning, she decided to confront him. The swimming had gone too far. She waited for him to come splashing in around 2 or 3 a.m. like he always did. She sat up in bed, clinging to the sheet that she had pulled up to her worried, tight little face. He lay down beside her and he rubbed her belly as if he were trying to make it rounder. It felt wonderfully comforting.

"I think I'm going crazy," she whimpered, watching his hand go round her belly.

"I've never felt more alive, Squishy. The only thing I'm missing is being with you."

"I know," she said, feeling as if the whole ocean, underneath her, would burst through the floorboards and swallow her up.

"I have this dream," he said. "I have this dream that you're sitting on the deck watching me swim, instead of being holed up inside here with a cross look on your face. And you're dangling your long legs in the water ... yes, they are longer than you think, Squishy. And suddenly you can't stand it anymore, the lure of the sea is too great, it just explodes inside you and you let yourself down into the water. I find you and you find me ... and together we find that ... we swim the same way."

Her face had gone very white. She pressed her back into the pillow and breathed in gasps.

"I can't live here anymore," she said. "I want to move to the city. Please, let's move to the city. They have big restaurants there. You could be a chef in one of those places. You're good enough. I've been the one keeping you here because of my family, but you always wanted to go to the city. Let's go now."

His hand went limp on her belly. He got up and went to the window and for a long time he watched the moon setting over the water. "I'll never leave here," he said finally. "It wouldn't be natural."

"I hate what you naturally are!" she cried, tears streaming from her eyes.

"I'm sorry," he said.

CHAPTER 7: The Wild Side

He went out on the deck and slipped into the water. He didn't put on a diving tank or a mask. He just lowered himself into the sea ... floated on the surface for a moment, and then sank with the moon.

That was the last she saw of him. She sold the houseboat and she moved into the city to be as far from the water as she could get. She ate to give herself comfort and ballooned into the beach ball shape of her childhood. Losing him was like losing her life. She grieved and grieved but she couldn't get over him. She couldn't get over to the other side.

She took a course in gourmet cooking and got herself a job as a chef in a small downtown restaurant. Nobody noticed her except through her food, which just got better and better. The only thing was, she couldn't stand the sight or the smell of seafood. The odor made her sick, heart-sick, so heavy of spirit that she felt she would crash through the floor and take the weight of the whole world with her. It reminded her of the old life, the old skin she had shed, the floating house and her beloved husband—HER one and only HIS, who had disappeared under the silver sea. The smell would encircle her like a spirit, filling her with a wistful longing to tell her story, to open the albums she refused to touch, to drive down to the shore she had abandoned and dare not revisit.

It all came to the surface one day when she was called out of the kitchen by a charming English gentleman and his wife, who had just completed a veal scaloppine. Their appreciation came pouring out like a fountain of clear water: they praised her delicate flavors, her sweet herbal overtones and the tenderness of her meat. A lump gathered in her throat. He used to talk to her like that. How round and ripe they were, like two apples growing together on the same tree ....

"Well, thank you," she said over the breaks in her voice. "It is satisfying to cook a meal for two people who are so obviously meant for one another." She rubbed her hands nervously in her apron.

"We're two peas in a pod," said the woman. "It would kill us to be apart."

"By the way, do you have a seafood special?" inquired the charming English man.

Tears rushed to her eyes and spilled uncontrollably down her cheeks, and before she knew it she had thrown her arms wide open and was announcing to the whole restaurant:

"No, I do NOT have a seafood special! I did, but I don't anymore!" Howling, she ran out the front door and into the street.

That night, she drove back down to the coast and sat on the rocky shore, a stone's throw from the old houseboat that now belonged to a noisy family with two rude children. She stared out at the water as the moon rose behind her, and the next morning she was gone. Only her clothes remained, strewn like old skin on the slimy rocks.

CHAPTER 7: The Wild Side

CHAPTER 7: The Wild Side

"She stared out at the water as the moon rose behind her, and the next morning, she was gone. Only her clothes remained, strewn like old skin on the slimy rocks."

The image that haunts me from this story is the wife on the rocks, going back to join her husband in the sea. I can understand her yearning for the other half that's down there, in a watery element that is more home than land.

I've held tight to this corporate persona because it has kept me, literally, grounded. The job gave me an identity, a direction and a future, but I never felt any real passion for it. It kept me sealed off from my own depths, which was useful because I didn't want to slip back into the old self. I was dreamy, addictive, lost and utterly lacking in direction. I could have so easily dissipated. It was hell to return to this stark, inhospitable, troubled world. I developed a sort of "grin and bear it mentality" which would explain my hard, defensive crust.

I reel in horror when I think of shedding my skin like she did and going down into that primal sea. But there's a part of me down there, a part I want to reclaim. A lot has changed since I left school. I'm pursuing something this time ... going in with my eyes open.

CHAPTER 8

Waiting

CHAPTER 8: Waiting

July 18

I got the job at Silvano's and I've been working for a while, adapting to a new routine. I'm keeping the vow I made to myself: no drinking with the staff after hours, no partying, no dating staff members.

Last night the artist (the one known as "the Prince"—his actual name is Bruno Riccio) came in for dinner. You wouldn't believe what a big deal people made. You would think God had arrived. What's with this guy? So he's a partner, so he's rich, so his relatives are Italian aristocrats, so he can afford to do nothing but paint and be admired. So-the-hell-what?

I've looked at his art a lot in the last few weeks. First I just felt its impact—bold and passionate and childlike in a street-smart, "screw you" sort of way. Then I ignored it, but now it's starting to bother me. It's too harsh, too fantastic, too overstated. And did I mention egotistical? Where does he get off painting so huge, like he's daring everyone to try and outsize him?

Sandy (one of the lovelier waiters) was gushing over his paintings the other night, saying how sensitive they were. I laughed and said, "There isn't a sensitive bone in this guy's body. He's all sharp edges." She gave me an arched look and said, "Al, you have no idea how gentle he is." The she swept up her tray and sallied off.

Fine. I gritted my teeth and prepared myself for a long night. At 8 he showed up, this suave Italian wearing a white linen shirt, a gray Armani suit and a woman on his arm. No mere mortal either, I hasten to add. A dark queen, a chocolate-skinned Nefertiti. She wore a broad pearl choker around her perfect throat, and an off-the-shoulder black dress. He was, of course, the perfect gentleman in every detail. Perfectly manicured, right down to the cuff links and the white rose in his lapel. He stole the attention of the whole restaurant. Everyone's whispering "Who's that?" and we have to explain, "He's the ARTIST," while we pass out accolades.

I hate that guy. Maybe it wouldn't bother me so much if I had some ground of my own to stand on. But I'm just a waiter. A servant. A functionary. Okay, so I'm jealous, so sue me. I'm just thankful I didn't have to wait on him. I didn't have to stand there and say, "Yes, fine sir. Would you like your talent before your riches? No problem. A goddess on the side? Certainly sir, whatever you wish. Anything for dessert?"

CHAPTER 8: Waiting

FROM THE DESK OF A. SEEKER

I was really griping when I found "The Broken Pot." Some customer had put it under a table leg to balance a wobbly table. I sympathize with the table.

CHAPTER 8: Waiting

The Broken Pot

A plain old pot, that's me. A black lacquered, fat-bellied pottery pitcher, useful for pouring milk into cereal dishes or water into house plants. No, not very impressive. Not something you would want to put on display or use to pour a very fine wine.

In fact, you can't find a more ordinary chap than me. I'm not even sure I am a chap. I might be a gal for all I know. I have very little personality, really.

Now, don't get me wrong, I'm not putting myself down. I did that once, and I'll never do it again. On the days when I sat on a shelf in the kitchen, I used to stare out at the china cabinet in the dining room. My mistress had a marvelous collection of porcelain and crystal from all over the world. I couldn't take my eyes off it. My eyes were always over there. At night I would dream of being a porcelain vase, of holding roses, orchids or gladiolas with everybody's eyes on me. When I woke, I would remind myself that I had some worth too. I might not have beauty but I have a function in the household and that's got to be worth something, surely. But my value seemed so lowly next to theirs that all my little attempts to argue myself into a feeling of self-worth didn't amount to a hill of beans in the end.

My eyes were so often over there on the display case that one day I ended up quite beside myself and I don't mean in a figurative way. Quite suddenly, I found myself standing OUTSIDE my own fat pitcher body. I couldn't get back in. It was as though my body had said, "Okay, you don't like being in here, then you stay out there." Now I wanted back in. "Hey, let me in!" I cried, knocking at my pottery walls, but all gates were closed to me. I watched as my beautiful black glaze lost its luster and fire. Eventually, my mistress stopped noticing me. She would just grab me unconsciously, shove me under the tap with her eyes out the window, dump water on her plants, and have done with me. Things being what they are, our combined lack of care inevitably met one day. I slipped out of her hand and shattered at her feet.

It was terrible. I don't like even thinking about it, really I don't. There I was, outside myself, looking down at the shattered pieces that had been me. I was suddenly so confused. Where was I? Who was I? Just a bunch of shards, getting swept into a bag with fish skins and chicken bones.

I floated around, a detached pitcher soul, going from vase to vase, trying to get inside them and being refused, over and over again. Finally, one vase did let me in—an old oriental urn who stood poised on her own carved table in the corner. I had admired her more than all the other porcelain. She was the queen of vases, an old and stately grandmother. She invited me to come and stay inside her, which

CHAPTER 8: Waiting

wasn't an easy feat. Imagine me trying to squeeze my poor, fat pitcher spirit down through her thin, fragile neck! Well, for once I didn't break anything, and I curled up in her warm recesses; got set for a little sleep.

"My dear, what have you done with yourself?" she asked in her husky, craquelure voice. "You're welcome to stay of course, but you do know, I hope, that this isn't where you belong."

"Yes, I know," I said. I was too tired to make up any excuses for myself; only relieved to find a place to stay. I admitted to her that I had once had a perfectly good body, but I abandoned it because it was so ugly, plain, and functional.

Did she ever laugh! She laughed so hard I thought she was going to crack, and she did just a little. New sepia lines ran down the inside of her body, which was so fragile you could see the warm, golden light coming in from outside.

"Why are you laughing?" I asked.

"Because my dear, all my life I've wanted a function! I never had one, though I must admit, I never thought I'd get one this way!"

"You have no function at all?"

"No, my dear. I'm purely ornamental."

I was a bit horrified. "Why were you made then?"

"Search me."

Well now, that put me into quite a spin. Why would anyone go to so much trouble to make a perfectly useless vase into such an exquisite work of art? Wouldn't their time have been better spent on something a bit more FUNCTIONAL?

"Doesn't it bother you that you have no function? Don't you feel kind of … worthless?"

"My dear young pitcher, I will have you know that I am the most valuable vase in this whole collection. You cannot even possibly conceive of my worth." Her tone had acquired a sharp edge, and I realized that I had put her quite off.

I fell silent. I felt small. I felt hard. I grew angry. I wanted to shout, "How did you get to be so valuable? What did you ever do to deserve becoming such an objét d'art? I did nothing but work my whole life and nobody decorated me. I've got no value at all!" My poor spirit began to twitch, flinging itself this way and that inside the vase.

"Young fellow," she said finally, "You are giving me a stomach ache. I would like to tell you to leave, but I feel sorry for you because you have no place in this world,

CHAPTER 8: Waiting

no place at all. Not only are you without a function, but you have no place to dwell—neither in the past nor the future. Your only hope is here in the present, in me. If you are going to stay I must insist that you relax."

With that, she turned her attention away from me. I wasn't at all comfortable in her pear-shaped belly. It was too confining and delicate a space. Oh, how I longed to be back in my old fat pitcher shape. How wretched I was in there! She was right, though. I had no other place to go.

So I did something that is not worthy of me, I know, but I couldn't help it. I mean, you have to do something when you're all holed up in a place where even dying is out of the question. I got to feeling that this old lady had some nerve talking to me like that. Who did she think she was, anyway? A basically useless ornament who had no right to enjoy the attention that flowed to her from everyone. "There is no justice in this world," I growled. "Why should a useless vase have everything, and a hardworking, functional pitcher like me have nothing? I spent my whole life working—for what?" As I ground on, I noticed that I had started to chip away at a little sepia vein running down the side of one wall. It felt good to get inside her cracks, and after a while it became an occupation to see if I could actually make a fissure wide enough to slip through. I tried one crack, then another, and then I got the idea that maybe I would go all the way around and collapse her from the inside. Haha!

The fateful day arrived when my mistress came along and reached for her precious old vase. I watched as the shadow of the dust cloth ever so gently caressed the outer surface of the ornament. She shifted it a little to the left in order to dust the table, and to her horror, the vase fell apart, just disintegrated right there and then on the display table.

Suddenly both our spirits were released. I couldn't see the old lady when she departed, but I felt her relief. It expanded through the room and settled on everything like sparkling snow. I realized what an extraordinary effort it had been for her to hold her fragile self together all those years, and now that she was released she could finally get that bit of rest she needed before going on to the next accomplishment.

She flew off happily, I don't know where. As for me, I was made of denser stuff. I went from place to place in the house, settling in this or that corner—an ashtray, a candy-dish, a plant pot. Needless to say, if I had any worth before, I had none now. I was nothing but spirit sludge, old jug sludge, completely undeserving of any notice whatsoever.

Then one day, from my seat in a candle holder, I noticed that the mistress of the house had taken out her paints and her canvasses. She hadn't painted for some

CHAPTER 8: Waiting

time, years perhaps, but she had become inspired again. She took out her oils and her palette, and began to mix the colors, and all at once I got the strangest sensation, just the strangest sensation, like I was being drawn into something more powerful than me. I spiraled around and around, carried by the force of a current. It was a happy sensation, and a welcome one—an ecstatic and painful pulling in.

When I came to my senses, I found myself looking out from a place that I couldn't quite capture entirely. I could see my mistress scrutinizing me. She studied me from every angle and I must say I felt quite exposed. I had never been looked at that way, and I was quite in love with her when it was all over. A devoted dog of a pitcher was I! Then other people came and looked at me, and after that, I was put in the dark. Some time later, the light returned and I found myself in the hall. To my great good fortune, a mirror hung opposite me, so I could see what I had become.

There I was, back in my old fat pitcher body, captured in a painting where I had been fondly placed on a table full of pitchers—large and small pitchers, pitchers holding flowers and water and ashes, pitchers plain and decorated, ornamental and functional, with and without apparent worth ... all crowded together ... and in our center, shining like a light and speaking for pitchers everywhere, stood the old oriental vase—the very soul of refreshment!

CHAPTER 8: Waiting

CHAPTER 8: Waiting

"If I had any worth before, I had none now. I was nothing but spirit sludge, old jug sludge, completely undeserving of any notice whatsoever."

Lately I've been fighting the feeling that I'm totally useless, just like the discarnate pitcher spirit, without value of any kind. This state of uselessness seems to be going on forever. I'm earning a living, but I don't have a life. Like the jug, I don't identify with my functional self, the one who goes to work every day. Being a waiter doesn't have any worth for me. I'm neither here nor there, just lying around in an ashtray. Ha!

The story suggests that the quest will eventually lead to some larger purpose. It's interesting that when the pitcher makes the transition to the canvas, he remains an ordinary pitcher. The only thing that's changed is that he has been appreciated by someone with an artistic eye. I'm reminded of Tony, the owner of Silvano's. He's not doing anything extraordinary in running a restaurant, but the guy is passionate about what he's doing. He sounds like a priest when he talks about Silvano's. "When the people come here, it's like a communion, no? We give them a little bread, a little wine, a little music ... we make them happy ... no?"

Back in the ashtray ... I have to believe that I will eventually be drawn into some greater purpose. But so far, I don't see any artist coming along with her paints ....

So I wait. Maybe I'll never be anything more than a waiter. Waiting forever. I'm trying to arrive at some peace with that.

CHAPTER 9

Seeing the Treasure Within

CHAPTER 9: Seeing the Treasure Within

August 3

Caroline came over last night. She gave me a card: a watercolor of a misty seascape with a rainbow hanging like a siren over the cliffs. Inside, she had written:

> *I am the daughter of Earth and Water,*
> *And the nursling of the Sky;*
> *I pass through the pores of ocean and shores:*
> *I change, but I cannot die.*

It's from a poem called "The Cloud" by the Romantic poet, Percy Bysshe Shelley. I read the card while she watched me, her beautiful dark eyes shining. I appreciated the encouragement, the reminder that this change isn't going to kill me, and especially the knowledge that she cares. Caroline seems to understand a lot that we don't speak about. There is chemistry between us but neither of us has said anything. We're enjoying being friends. There is control here, and a certain restraint which is giving rare power to the relationship.

We went out for a walk in the park, and ended up getting dessert at a little coffee place nearby. It was a warm night, full of flower scent, round moon rising over the trees. Intensely romantic. I admitted my fear of going backwards, returning to old waters. I told her about my addictive tendencies and the policy I made to stay on track. She said that some of the nineteenth century romantic poets had similar tendencies. Samuel Taylor Coleridge got hooked on opium. "Maybe a desire to escape just comes with the territory. It's part of your GENIUS," she said. I thought she was teasing me, but she said, "No, really, if you want to escape, maybe it's because you know a better world. So bring it HERE."

After we had coffee, I walked Caroline home. She lives only a few blocks away—rents the second and third floor of a house. We said goodnight. She lingered on the steps, and I'm thinking, Come on, here's your chance A., but I didn't make a move and neither did she.

August 30

I'm intensely lonely, almost overwhelmed by a sense of deprivation. Why do I feel so deprived? I have to remind myself that I have consciously cloistered myself in an attempt to focus on my art. Ha! I keep hearing my Dad saying, "You're wasting your time," and he might be right. How do you focus on doodling? How do you give value to what you've always seen as a waste of time, a "goof-off"?

CHAPTER 9: Seeing the Treasure Within

I'm doing everything in my power to stay on the path. I work from 5 to midnight. I come home. I go to sleep. I get up in good time and draw in the afternoon. I sit by the window with my sketch pad, trying to produce something. But it makes me sick to draw, physically nauseous. I'm staring at this blank page, gazing down into my own emptiness, the futility of my effort.

Maybe I should have taken that job. At this age (I'm closing in on 40) there are so many "shoulds" I haven't fulfilled. I should have money, a car, a wife, a job, some kids, a retirement savings plan, an insurance policy, a cottage by the lake ... the list goes on and on. I've got nothing. And no ability to draw to boot.

10:58 pm

This afternoon, the most amazing thing happened. I was sitting there trying to draw, and my thoughts were wandering all over the place, finding all my unsatisfied desires, wants and needs ... and suddenly I saw what I had been "doodling." For the first time, I actually SAW what I was drawing:

A man in the dark is opening a treasure chest, and he's practically blinded by the light that's coming from inside.

CHAPTER 9: Seeing the Treasure Within

FROM THE DESK OF A. SEEKER

Only hours after I drew the picture, I found this story in the laundry room of our building. It might have floated in through the window for all I know. It was so strange. I had the impression that my queries had been heard and answered, as if the walls had been listening. Is this "synchronicity"?

CHAPTER 9: Seeing the Treasure Within

The Treasures of the Mine

There once was a clerk who was just about the grimmest person anyone would ever want to meet. He hardly spoke, he hung his head low, he sniffed and coughed and complained about bugs. He hated his job as a bookkeeper, but he didn't have much education, and, well, his father had worked as a bookkeeper and his father before him, so that was his lot. Not a helluva lot as far as he was concerned, but who was he to question what bones God saw fit to throw him?

One day on his way to town, the clerk passed an old woman sitting by an old stone well on the edge of his property. The well had dried up long ago, during the days when his grandfather owned the land.

"Go downs there," the old woman croaked. She pointed a gnarled finger down the well.

The man ignored her. He had been coughing all night, and his lungs were on fire. He figured she must be some figment of his literally fevered imagination, so he carried on his way.

The next day, when he made his way to work, there she was again, sitting hunched on the edge of the well. She had long white hair, eyes as blue as crystals, and a drooping, crooked nose.

"Go downs there," she said.

He felt a little better today, so he stopped and spoke with her. "What's down there?" he asked.

"Your mine," she said.

"You must be mistaken. There's no mine down there."

"Oh, yes there is," she said with such certainty that he was forced to seriously consider what she could possibly mean. After a few moments, he asked, "What kind of mine are you talking about?"

"YOUR mine."

"Yes, but you see, it's not a mine, it's a well."

"Your MINE," she said, giving him a big smile. The few teeth she had in her head were brown as bark.

He rubbed his beard. Even with a clear mind he would have had a hard time making sense of this. What was she talking about? Was it possible that she knew something he didn't? Was there something precious down there? Gold? Silver, perhaps? Copper ore? No, that was impossible. Not on his land. Not in his life.

CHAPTER 9: Seeing the Treasure Within

"The only kind of mine I would have is one that would blow up in my face," he thought to himself.

With that sullen thought, he continued on his way. But all day long, and all night long, he couldn't take his mind off the old woman at the well. By morning, he decided that he had to further investigate the matter.

He got himself equipped with good rope and went to the well at the edge of his property. The old woman was not there. He tied his rope to a young fir tree that stood beside it, dropped the rope down the well and climbed to the bottom. To his surprise, he found himself standing at the end of a long passageway. At the other end, a blue light flickered on a damp stone wall. He followed the passageway to a T intersection, and then he had to make a choice: whether to go down the passage to the right or to the left. Both ended in blue lights. He turned right, and went to the end of the hall, where he came to another T with a blue light. This time he turned left, and so he went, turning this way and that way until he didn't know where he was or how to get back. "Why didn't I just stick to one direction?" he wailed. "How am I ever going to get out of here?"

With panic rising, he ran through hall after hall, but they all looked the same. Eventually he could run no more. He weakened, staggered, and fell upon the dirt floor, weeping. When he opened his eyes, he noticed that the passage he occupied had one unique feature. Unlike the others, the hall trailed off into darkness. He saw no blue light at the far end. Where did it lead? To follow it into the shadows was his only hope. He got up shakily and felt his way along the wall as it narrowed and descended and shrank into a tunnel no bigger than a crawl space. He got on his knees and went in. The passage twined downwards like a root, twisting into the bowels of the earth. He had no idea where he was going, but he did know he would never be able to turn around and go back.

Finally, the passage levelled off and opened up. He stood and walked down a wide hall. Ahead, a ghoulish green light spilled into the passage from one side. Tentatively, he walked towards the light and turned into the entrance of a cave. Brilliant sulfurous torches were attached to its walls. In the middle of the room, a gnome sat on a stack of thick, oversized books with his fist thrust into his chin. He wore a green tunic, and he had a long gray beard, an obscenely large nose, a tiny body and huge feet. He looked up at the clerk without moving his head, in a manner that was decidedly bored and even a little disgusted.

"So what have you brought me this time?" he asked.

"Brought you? Nothing," said the man.

"Nothing? Are you telling me that you spent everything on nothing?"

"I don't know what you're talking about," said the man. "I haven't got anything to spend."

CHAPTER 9: Seeing the Treasure Within

"What? You haven't got ANYTHING? What have you been doing with your life?" the gnome shrieked.

"Working," said the clerk, annoyed. "Trying to make a living."

The gnome ignored him and hopped off the stack of books. He circled the clerk in an attempt to investigate his pockets, which was not an easy feat, given the fact that he was shorter than the pockets and he had to jump up to peer in.

"Where's your happiness?" he screamed, hanging off the back pocket of his trousers. "You must have some of that."

"I'm happy enough," said the man.

"Well, where is it?"

"Are you looking for something in particular?"

"Of course I'm looking for something in particular!" shouted the gnome. He let go of the pocket and tumbled down to the ground. "I see no evidence of happiness anywhere. Where's your treasure?"

"I told you, I don't have any. I've never been rich."

"So you've spent all your gems? You don't even have a trinket? Nothing at all?"

"No, I tell you!"

"You MUST have something!!!"

"I don't know what you're looking for!"

"I'll show you what I'm looking for!" The gnome scrambled over to the stack of books and pushed them aside, revealing a trap door. He pulled on the latch and disappeared down the hole. The man, thoroughly befuddled, descended down a series of rickety steps that led to a small, musty cellar. The moment his head came under the upper floor, he could smell the familiarity of the room below. The gnome went around opening boxes stuffed with treasures from lives gone by. In the photographs and paintings he recognized the woman he had loved, time after time, through all the changes of fashion. He saw the seashells that he had collected through all his childhoods on countless shores. He saw the carefully prized letters of his children and his grandchildren; the dolls and the games they had left behind. It was all there—all the treasures of his time. No bitterness, no regret, just treasure. Everything he had ever cherished in all of his lives.

"That's it," said the gnome, rubbing his hands. "That's what you brought back before. Now come along." He turned and stamped up the stairs.

"Wait," said the man. "Let me stay here awhile. Let me remember all this."

CHAPTER 9: Seeing the Treasure Within

"Remember? All I care about is the treasures you have NOW," the gnome snapped.

Now. What did he treasure now? He was, by his own decree, a nose-to-the-grindstone sort of person, a loyal, hardworking man. Did he treasure anything? Surely he treasured his wife and his little girl? Well, sure he did, but how? He honestly didn't know. And how had he shown his love? To whom? Was it possible that his wife was the same cherished woman whose many faces he recognized in all the paintings and photographs? Why couldn't he answer that? Why didn't he know? Was he so blind? And what about his little daughter? Who was she to him? What games did they play that he would cherish for all time? What shore did he walk upon now, collecting shells?

"Just one more minute," he pleaded, falling to his knees. "Let me sort this out." But the gnome wasn't having any of it. "Come along NOW," he commanded. The man had no choice but to collect himself and follow the little fellow up the stairs.

The gnome shut the cellar door, sat on his pile of books again and dropped his chin on his fist.

"What do I do now?" asked the man. "Where do I go?"

"You tell me," said the gnome. "I don't know what the point would be of another life. You've been getting poorer and poorer, but you've never brought me nothing before. You didn't treasure one moment from the time you were born to the time you died."

"But I haven't died," said the man.

"What? That's impossible. How did you get down here if you didn't die?"

"I climbed down."

"Eh?"

"An old woman pointed the way."

The gnome frowned. "White hair, eyes like two blue crystals, long crooked nose?"

"That's her," said the man.

"Oh, for heaven's sake. She's supposed to stay put."

"Who is she?"

"She's a fir tree."

"What?"

"She's obviously taken a liking to you. She'll kill herself doing that. But it's the nature of fir trees. Every now and then, they fall in love with a person and when

CHAPTER 9: Seeing the Treasure Within

they do, they show them their roots. You're a lucky man. Are you sure you're not dead?"

"No, I swear. I'm not dead."

"Well, she's given you a second chance. Best get back straight away."

"How?" asked the man, but no sooner were the words out of his mouth than he awoke by the well. When he raised his head off the ground, he saw the fir sapling, growing right in front of his nose. She looked quite dry and sickly, and he noticed that she was growing very close to the well. Too close to thrive. He put his arms around her and kissed her on her bristles. Then he went home, got a spade, and returned to the well to transplant the tree. Gently, he carried her to the edge of the forest, and gave her a place in the sun where the soil was good and she could see him coming and going. "Well might you see," he said to her, "for well I will always be." Then he went off to work as a clerk, the happiest fellow in the world. He never made any more money than anyone else in his family, but a richer man you will never meet.

CHAPTER 9: Seeing the Treasure Within

CHAPTER 9: Seeing the Treasure Within

"So what have you brought me this time?" asked the gnome.
"Brought you? Nothing," said the man.

I can imagine the clerk's confusion. He goes down into the mine hoping to find some treasure for himself, and he's confronted by a gnome who only wants to see what treasure HE has to offer. I'm reminded of what Caroline said about the orphan, about going after something that needs you to make IT living.

I read recently that in the 1920's corporate America consciously set out to create an insatiable consumer who would buy buy buy ... causing us to feel constantly unhappy, discontented, DEPRIVED if we didn't have the latest new car or fashion. It was actually called the "organized creation of dissatisfaction."

You know that bumper sticker that reads, "Whoever dies with the most toys WINS"? That's it in a nutshell. We're driven to accumulate all this stuff so that we can feel we've earned our place under the sun. So we can throw off this terrible feeling of being inadequate, unworthy of the space we occupy. Is it true? Can we buy our way to heaven with our toys? How many points do we need? Will St. Peter take credit cards?

The gnome wasn't interested in the man's points. He didn't know about advertising. All he saw was a man who kept dying with less and less. So what makes up our treasure? When I look away from my lacks to what I cherish ... health, friendship, freedom, family, the means to survive, a sense of beauty, a sense of wonder ... I see no end to the bounty. It's invisible because it's underneath us, supporting us. But how often do we think, "Wow, I have the ability to breathe! Isn't that wonderful!" My Aunt Helen, who has emphysema, once said, "Believe me, there is no hunger in the world like the hunger for air."

Like the clerk, I feel blessed to have come down to this place through the intervention of something other than loss: call it love, or serendipity or the whim of a fir tree. There is so much to be grateful for. I have felt so little gratitude in my life, but I feel it now. It's right here, all around me, enfolding me ... embracing everything.

CHAPTER 10

Getting Naked

CHAPTER 10: Getting Naked

A Seeker's Journal

September 25

It's happening. I'm starting to shed old skins. It's not just the corporate persona I'm peeling off. The layers go deeper than that. Under the media production guy in a suit is another guy in a suit, the compliant worker, and under that, the good student, and the obedient son: all personas I wore for the purpose of pleasing others and getting credits in the world. It's beginning to matter less and less what people think of me, though I have to admit, I'm avoiding social occasions. It's a little awkward to go out naked. No matter how comfortable you are in your own skin, people don't necessarily like to see you in it. I found that out the other night at a party, when someone asked me, "What do you do?" and I said, "I'm waiting." One guy sneered, "What for? Godot?" and walked away.

I'm not throwing anything away. I'm sorting, trying to figure out what I want and what I don't want. I don't want to be dependent on some organization for my survival. I don't want to be willing to compromise everything I care about just to stay afloat. I want to take responsibility for myself and the decisions I make. I want to pursue something, make some kind of contribution. I want to rediscover beauty and joy and pleasure in my work—give something back, make a difference, however small. The world has so many needs and there's so little time. I feel this urgency to find my calling and get on with it. But I'm still trying to figure that out.

On the weekend, I went over to Caroline's house and she showed me a fundraising video she produced for the Women's Shelter. She did it on her own time, using equipment from in-house. I guess she had Cadwell's approval. It's really admirable work—she's a good storyteller. But I have to admit, I was kind of down and I didn't offer the appreciation she deserved. I wished I could have given her more. I sat in the living room like a big, stupid rock while she got up to get the tea.

Finally, I said, "Am I boring?"

She said, "No, you're just being."

"What kind of a being?"

Christopher came into the room. "Boring," he said.

Ha. The wisdom of a child.

CHAPTER 10: Getting Naked

FROM THE DESK OF A. SEEKER

I found this story at the dentist's office. It was in a clear folder of amusing pieces his customers had written. The folder was titled "Pick Me Ups," and my eye went straight to "Old Woman's Hill."

CHAPTER 10: Getting Naked

Old Woman's Hill

There once was a woman who wore layers and layers of clothing: shirts and skirts, sweaters and coats, hats and trousers, blouses and boots of every imaginable color, shape and size.

She wore everything she had ever been given, all at the same time, and she never took her garments off. Sometimes a layer would just slough off, after growing threadbare due to weather and wear. The woman had no preferences for this shade or that style. She loved all her clothes the same. In fact, she got so attached to her layers that you couldn't talk her out of one scarf or mitten, no matter how hot the day or persuasive your reasoning. She wouldn't give anything up. She would, however, take on new stuff, and, indeed, the best way to become her friend was to offer her a piece of apparel. She would seize it, put it on and display it proudly no matter how worn, sodden, or smelly. She made it all her own.

I would like to tell you something about her face but it was hard to get a look at her through all the clothes she wore. Rumor had it she had short brown hair, bright brown eyes, and somewhat pointy white teeth. To verify that rumor, you would have to peer down a dark tunnel of clothes and that would not be advisable because the weight of her clothes had made her scratchy and snappish. The only way to make her happy (and ensure not being bitten) was to give her something colorful. That would lighten her load.

Day and night, night and day, she looked for clothes and begged for clothes and sometimes even robbed for clothes until she became so weighed down that she could hardly walk. One hot summer afternoon, while making her way down a country road, she stumbled and fell. Unable to get up under her own weight, she went to sleep on that very spot. When people passed, they commented on what a clever idea it was to make a big mound out of colorful fabric. The town needed a nice hill, and as time went by, people threw all their old clothes onto it. The hill grew larger and larger until one day, the children in the village came to play on the top. Before long their parents built them a playground there, and they filled the air with their laughter.

Time passed, and more time passed, and then one day, the woman woke up. She could hear muffled laughter high above her but she was stuffed so far down in her hill of clothes that she could not move her arms or her legs. Thinking very small, she began to worm her way out of her garments. It took a huge amount of concentration, but she managed to wriggle one arm out of a sleeve, and then the other. Then she pulled her legs out of her layers of pants and skirts, and after that, she shrank down through the neck of all her shirts, sweaters and jackets. Finally, naked as a possum, she burrowed a tunnel up to the top of the hill. She

CHAPTER 10: Getting Naked

popped her head out, and wonders of wonders, there was the sky stretched above her, bluebell blue, with the golden sun bobbing in the center and the children laughing on their swings.

She wasn't a young woman anymore, but for the first time she felt a twinge of happiness. "Oh, wouldn't it be fun to go and play with the children," she thought. She began to wriggle out of her hole and had nearly come right out of her mound when she realized that she didn't have a stitch on! "Clothes to wear, oh my, I better find something to wear," she muttered to herself, and turned around in her mound, moon to the sun. Down she went again, rummaging about for something to don. She looked here and she looked there, burrowing through the whole mound, but do you think that she could decide on what to wear? No! Not on your life!

The search went on for days. She burrowed tunnels up and down, from side to side, and from here to there, but she still couldn't settle on a thing to wear. At last, she gave up. She knew she would never be able to decide. She had far too many options and she couldn't narrow any of them down. She would have to wear it all or nothing. Rather than putting the weight back on, she decided to wear nothing at all.

She made her way back to the top of the hill and she popped her head out as she had done before. She watched the children swing like bells under the golden sun, and listened to them laugh, which was music to her ears. She couldn't have enough of their laughter. It gave her a happy feeling without any weight at all. After a while she forgot about her craving for clothes, and Nature took its course, providing for her as Nature will.

If you happen to visit that hill today, you will think that it is just an ordinary hill with a swing set, a sandbox and a slide on the top. But after fooling around there for some time, you will notice that the grass grows out of an especially colorful, fibrous soil. When you crouch down to have a look, you will see that it is actually made up of threads of fabric.

Around this time you will probably get the feeling that you are being watched, so you'll turn around and you'll see her, popping her head out of her hole, her bright brown eyes piercing you through. You will think, "Oh, it's just a groundhog," but then you will have a start because she will say to you as clear as the day, "Hello, welcome to my hill!" You will suddenly feel drowsy, and before you know it, you will be stretched out on the green grass with your ear to the ground, dreaming. When you come to, you will know her whole story and there she will be, looking at you with her sharp brown eyes. She will say: "Yes, everything you dreamed is true," and then she'll chuckle and duck back in her hole. You will go home like I did, saying you met the old woman who lives in the hill, which everyone who has forgotten their childhood will tell you is nothing but pure fabrication.

CHAPTER 10: Getting Naked

CHAPTER 10: Getting Naked

"'Clothes to wear, oh my, I better find something to wear,' she muttered to herself, and turned around in her mound, moon to the sun."

I've been searching in earnest for an identity, something to wear out there. But as I read this story, I started to think that maybe the struggle to find clothes is giving me a lot of unnecessary grief. Maybe I don't need to put anything on just now. Maybe it's okay to be naked for a while, go underground, hibernate. Nature does it, why shouldn't we?

When I allow myself to admit it, I am actually enjoying this state of rest. It's a state of possibility, a fascinating place to be. In this process of change, I'm not sure we can engineer the new form. I think there's a time to wait, to enjoy non-being as much as being. So that's what I'm doing right now. Cycling, enjoying the fall, tasting the colors, feeling the textures, remembering what it felt like to be a child playing in the schoolyard, at a time when the world was new and drenched in wonder.

CHAPTER 11

Down to the Core

CHAPTER 11: Down to the Core

A Seeker's Journal

March 2

After a winter of doing basically nothing, I started to draw again a couple of months ago. I've been drawing energetically, like there is all this fuel inside me. I've stopped censoring what I'm drawing and I'm paying much more attention to what's coming out. It's all violent, heavy-metal-type stuff. Every time I draw something soft and lyrical it makes me uneasy. I instinctively want to kill it or turn it into something hard.

There's a war in me, a war between two powers: the hard and the soft. The hard part of me is embodied in my Dad, the frustrated soldier who missed having a war to fight in his generation. He found his outlet in Phys Ed and turned it into a kind of preparatory base camp. He didn't let down the militia persona at home, either. He was forever with his whistle and his stop watch—barking commands at us. Do this, do that. We were on a schedule, meal times were set-in-stone times. His philosophy was delivered to us in palatable little aphorisms, like "eat or be eaten," "play to win," "vanquish the weak," "win the race," "don't be a loser," "run like hell," "get on the winning side." There were thousands of them. These are the voices that keep me sweating at night, thinking, you loser, get a life. Echoed by my Dad on the telephone, "You're pedaling backwards, Albert. Why in hell didn't you take that training job? Now you're back to where you started, with no future." He has no time for the artist. He tells me I'm soft.

Caroline says that in folklore there is this repetitive theme of the three sons: the first two are hard—they grow up to be merchants and warriors, following in their father's footsteps. The third son is the mother's son. He's a poet and a dreamer. His brothers think he's a fool, but he's loved by women and by the creatures of the natural world. In the end, he wins the heart of the princess and the kingdom too.

So I'm back to the question, "What is power?" Is it defined by control or by caring? Is it hard or soft? When I look at my drawings, and the stories I tell, they're all of the superman genre. The heroes might be saviors, but first and foremost, they're tough. They don't vanquish their enemies, they demolish them. They burn on revenge. My stories are not different than most of the adventure stories in our culture. We idolize the strong. We are embarrassed by the weak. We teach our children to lose their weakness, their vulnerability. In the process, they lose everything that is beautiful and sweet about them, and you know, that's what makes me sick. That's what causes me to revolt, to not want to look at my work.

I hate that the strong overcome the weak. I hate that my sister Alison has to live in a world where she is labelled "disabled" and warehoused away in a "group home" because she can't read or write. I hate that nobody values her for who she is, that

CHAPTER 11: Down to the Core

nobody speaks to her at social occasions, much less learns anything from her. She's an amazingly sensitive, beautiful, maybe even wise woman whose presence here on this planet and in our lives is pure Mystery. I hate that she isn't recognized.

... It just occurred to me that I am hardened by my hate. It makes me feel small and mean, like the troll. It doesn't give me any real power at all.

March 8

Yesterday, I laid all my stuff out on the living room floor, all the storyboards I've drawn in the last couple of years. I've been more productive than I thought. I addressed my work, saying: "Okay, if I can't change the story here, I'm gonna quit drawing." And I will. I am prepared to quit drawing altogether if I can't get something to come from the heart.

CHAPTER 11: Down to the Core

FROM THE DESK OF A. SEEKER

After I made that vow about drawing from the heart, I lost all motivation to draw. I was exhausted; couldn't seem to pull it together. Many dreams. A deep reordering of priorities was going on. I thought, Well, at least I'm not divided anymore. That's what I told my friend Hank, and knowing my penchant for collecting weird tales, he said, "Have I got a story for you!"

CHAPTER 11: Down to the Core

The Divided Man

There are two men living together. By living together, I mean really living together: as intimately as it is possible to live together. There is an outer man and an inner man and they share a single body and a single head. No one knows that there are two men in one body, but that's how it is.

Time goes on, and the differences begin to show. The outer man is a hard man: hard worker, hard driver, hard drinker, hard dealer. He's a man who wants results. The inner man is a soft man, an ideas chap. He digs around in the interior, gazing into Mystery, churning out poetry and reflections for no other reason than the wonder of life.

The outer man is the one who does commerce with the world. He is the one people want to work with and socialize with and be entertained by. He's a wealthy man with a lot of money and the means to make the world turn. The outer man used to acknowledge the inner man, but he has grown so large within the body that he has forgotten the other exists. The inner man finds himself going unheard and suffers from a feeling of uselessness. He begins to feel that the treasures he digs up aren't worth much to anyone, and so they lose their savor. He watches the outer man with increasing awe. He studies him and wishes that he could attract to himself a thimbleful of the interest that the outer man has for the world outside.

Then one night, the outer man has a party to celebrate his promotion to high office. Everyone arrives dressed to the nines. It is a black tie affair. The outer man receives his guests, sitting elegantly on the edge of the fountain in the back of his palatial mansion. Hundreds of people mill about in the garden, gathering up their drinks and food, and gravitating like a swirl of stars to the powerful man at the core.

The orchestra stops for a break, and all the people happen to inhale in the same breath. For an instant, time is suspended, and, to his own surprise, the inner man finds himself detaching from the outer. At first the guests see one man but then the man seems to split into two. Or is it one man? No, there is definitely another man. It's just hard to make him out because he doesn't have distinct edges. Oh yes, there he is, clad in a light blue sweater and sadly underdressed for the occasion. The outer man turns to the inner man, and, with cold disdain, he says, "I'm so glad to be free of you." The inner man starts to tremble. He whimpers, "Please take me back," but the outer man is a fortress with no door, and the inner man is shut out forever, knowing that the more he pleads, the more despicable he will be to his other half.

Before the guests have taken their next breath, the inner man is up on his feet. He begins to wobble out of the scene. The people whisper, "What kind of a man is that?" and indeed, after the music resumes, they conclude, "No man at all, nothing but a ghost." The crowd merges again, and the people resume their galactic dance to the powerful man who sits at the fountain.

The outer man feels a growing heaviness that makes it more and more difficult to move, or make conversation. Gradually, the swirling people find themselves drawn away to other attractions, and eventually he is forgotten altogether. He stays there, solidifying, while all the guests go home. The new day arrives. The winds and the storms come and tear away his elegant clothes ... and still he remains until all his concrete is exposed and the birds make a nest on his crown.

As for the inner man, he continues walking along the same course, becoming more and more immaterial. With rhythm and resolve, he begins to ascend into the sky, like a bird returning home. He does not need to stop and ask for directions, the highways of the sky are known. As he nears his home star, he becomes more and more excited about returning to the Source and being reunited with forgotten memories and possible futures. He breaks into a run, but for some strange reason, his strides do not advance him. In fact, he sees that he has been running in the same place for some time. He looks around to see that a silvery cord is attached to his back. It trails like a long spidery thread all the way down to earth. He can go no farther, he is at the end of his thread. He becomes angry. Why should he still be connected to that other fellow who rejected him in the first place? He would sever the cord with his teeth if he could, but it is too strong to be broken. So he pulls, with all his might, he pulls on that long silver cord.

The concrete man sitting on the fountain is moved: only slightly, mind you, but distinctly moved. Oh yes, he is quite sure of it. He knows he didn't move himself, his body is too stiff. It must have come from some outside force. Yet, he reflects, the movement did not come from outside, it came from within. How strange.
He waits, alert as a starving lion who sees motion in the grass. Once again he is tugged. Oh, yes, he is quite sure of it this time. To think that there might be some life in him after all, it is too much! Hope seeps through him, and with it, a terrible yearning.

Meanwhile, back in the heavens, the inner man is in quite a funk. Unable to detach himself from the other, he decides to go down and demand that the outer man let him go. Back he goes, all the way down to earth. It is a long, long journey.

The outer man sits by the fountain, waiting to be moved again, but nothing happens. Time goes by, and he remembers the moment. He lets it grow big in his mind. He cradles that hope, holding firm against the dark forces that tell him it was nothing but a phantom, immaterial as the memory of the inner man.

Then one night, the outer man wakes from a dreamless sleep to see the inner man standing before him. He wears the same old blue sweater and his face is weary and lined with impatience. But the outer man does not notice the inner man's hard face. Instead, he is looking at his hands, for he is holding a ball of silver twine, a shining sphere of starlight. "My brother, you've returned!" he exclaims, leaping up to embrace his friend. Before the inner man can utter a word, he has passed through the walls of the outer man and the two are one. The inner man returns to his rightful place at the edge of Mystery and the outer man promises never again to let him out of his sight. As for the shining sphere of starlight, it dances merrily around the man until his two selves are joined. Then it settles in his heart, and unravels a path to the stars.

CHAPTER 11: Down to the Core

CHAPTER 11: Down to the Core

"The movement did not come from outside, it came from within. How strange."

I'm a bit bothered that I identify so strongly with the concrete man, but the fact is, I do. I can feel exactly what it is like to sit there anticipating the next inner tug.

My mother and I used to go to church together every Sunday. My father never went. He would proudly say that the closest he ever got to a church was the parking lot. When I was twelve my Dad said, "You're old enough to make your own decision about church." I decided to quit going, not on spiritual grounds, but because I wanted to impress my Dad. It worked. He secretly congratulated me for making the decision. It was another step towards becoming a tough guy and moving away from my mother. After that, when my mother would go off to church with Alison, my Dad would call out, "Pray for us sinners!" and clap me on the back. Then we'd go out and throw ball.

But that tug in the concrete man is happening inside me, and maybe it's happening inside the world too; a melting at the center that moves outward and ultimately changes the course of the whole being.

I dreamt last night that I was asked to come to the bedside of a dying man. He was dying because he had swallowed concrete. He was filled from his head to his toes with the stuff. As it was drying, he was dying. He wanted me to tell him a story. In the room, all these women stood with their arms full of books. Nobody could find the right story. I knew the story he needed to hear. It wasn't in a book, it was alive in me. I sat down and as I began the story, tears ran down his face, and the tears kept the concrete from drying. Every time I shifted consciousness to another dream, or woke up, he would pull me back until I finished telling him the whole story. I don't know what happened to him, but I've been mourning him all day. Like I knew him. All these experiences are changing my concept of power. Power is the ability to soften, to feel, to flow. To become whole.

CHAPTER 12

Dream Fields

CHAPTER 12: Dream Fields

A Seeker's Journal

April 10

Yesterday morning I had a dream of a bee buzzing around in a field of flowers, following the bee line of his attractions. I woke up wondering, "Where is my dream field?" A simple question, but what did it mean? I thought about my field. What is my field? The answer came instantly. Illustration. Okay, so where do I find my field? Then it dawned on me: the children's bookstore. That's where my dreams are expressed. It's only a few blocks away—I go by it every day. I went down and started looking at children's illustrations. I bought some books, came home and pored over the artwork. It was really exciting spending time with those artists; like being with kin.

I started reading the stories. I liked some of them, but I was looking for something more, something that wasn't there. Then I realized what was missing. Adult content. I wanted adult content. I wanted to read stories and see illustrations that were drawn with a childlike spirit, but didn't censor or eliminate adult feelings, big ideas, big questions, radical notions. I thought about the work of Bruno Riccio. What made his art so compelling was that meld of childlike wonder and adult perspective. It was integrated.

That's what I want to do, I thought. I want to integrate the two perspectives! But there was more. I was just warming up. I thought, Wouldn't it be neat to illustrate a story so completely that it could be "read" like a children's picture book? No words, just pictures—childlike pictures drawn with so much sophistication and depth that they would speak to an adult audience? I got so excited I had to go outside and take a run on my bike just to siphon off some of the energy.

Now all I need is a story. A story about a true hero. Someone like my sister. Someone who isn't strong, someone who comes to the planet disabled, burned, broken-hearted, rejected, set back or lost, and still finds a way to happiness. That kind of character lives in us all. That's who I want to draw out.

CHAPTER 12: Dream Fields

FROM THE DESK OF A. SEEKER

I went to a storytelling gathering and heard "The Flammable Angel." I wanted to hear it again, I was so moved. I saw all the pictures clearly and in vivid detail. Afterwards, I asked the author if I could get a copy, and she sent it to me.

CHAPTER 12: Dream Fields

The Flammable Angel

There once was an angel named Patsy who got her wings burnt on the first day of the job. After that, she didn't want to be an angel anymore. Every morning, she hung around heaven and sulked while the other angels prepared to go down to the fiery earth, where they played their harps to comfort people in pain. The angels took pride in their ability to stand in the flames of human suffering and not get scorched. Most times their music went unheard; they just played their harps while the fires burned, happy to be angels and above things.

Patsy's wings were all crispy and blackened at the tips, and she had burnt her breast so badly that it hurt to fly. She had hardly approached earth when she went up in flames. Luckily, a big angel stepped in and snatched her out of the fire, but Patsy returned to heaven in a terrible mess. She had lost her harp, to say nothing of her dignity.

The other angels looked down on her and said: "Oh, isn't that terrible, there there dear," and, "You'll heal in time, you just rest now," but when Patsy wasn't looking they glanced at one another with raised eyebrows and wondered what business she had in heaven. Angels weren't supposed to get burnt. Oh, it happened on occasion that a very mature angel might take a little browning after overextending herself, but it usually took no more than a good night's rest for her wings to return to their dazzling snow-whiteness.

As for her peers, they didn't speak to Patsy at all. They scorned her, with the exception of a tiny angel named Cora. She sat with Patsy on the steps of the angelic temple while the other angels swept down the stairs and disappeared under white billowing clouds. She huddled close, like a little owl. Cora had been in heaven a long time, but she had not grown in greatness like the others. She had stayed small. She preferred to stay small; she said when you're small you can get into small places, and small fires can be put out.

Patsy hung her head. "Angels aren't supposed to be flammable, are they?"

"I don't think so," said Cora. "You're the first."

"Why was I made an angel if I can't do the work? I've got no reason for being here at all."

"Oh yes you do," said Cora. She picked off bits of Patsy's burnt wing tips and watched the singe float down through the clouds. "God put you here for a reason, even if we don't know what it is."

"What reason?"

Cora looked at her with widening round eyes. "Maybe you need to find out."

CHAPTER 12: Dream Fields

"You mean, from God?"

"Absolutely. Go right to the top."

They gazed over their shoulders at the towering purple mountain with the white spiral road that led to the palace where God lived. Right then and there, Patsy knew what to do.

During the time that it took for her wings to grow back, Patsy took short flights around her home colony, Cloud 9, in preparation for takeoff. She would need all her strength to fly through the windy region that separated the angelic realm from Mt. Divine. There, the tails of the four winds met and lashed the pilgrim with such force that only a very courageous angel with furious conviction could hope to make it through.

One morning, before any of the other angels had risen, Patsy headed off through the winds. She took quite a beating, but by midafternoon she had come out the other end, and there is no describing the gladness she felt when her foot finally touched solid (albeit, soft and cloudy) ground. She stumbled forward rubbing her stinging eyes, and for that reason, she didn't notice the huge green dragon who lay sleeping in the field with his chin on the road and his tail coiled around the base of the mountain. She bumped right into the side of his head!

The beast woke up with a start, reared back on his haunches, and roared. He sent a blast of fire across the road that scorched a swath of trees on the other side. Patsy yelped and sprang back in terror, but when the dragon saw who had disturbed his nap—an angel, and not much of a specimen at that—his yellow eyes rolled back in his head, and his chin came crashing down on the road. He had just started a new dream when he heard a tiny voice say:

"Pardon me, but I would like to get by, if you wouldn't mind. I need to see God."

He lifted his heavy head and yawned. "Ah yes, well you know the rules. Those who want to see God have to walk through fire first. I'm sure you're as excited as I am about your big test." His tone was decidedly sarcastic. He opened his jaws, let out a sigh of fire, and then dropped his chin back on the road.

Patsy crossed her arms and stood her ground. "If you expect me to walk through fire, I can't."

"Why not, pray tell?" The dragon opened an eye, which didn't even so much as flicker with interest.

"Because I'm flammable, that's why."

The dragon grinned, and then he began to chuckle, causing the mountain to teeter and totter dangerously. "Hehe, that's a good one. A FLAMMABLE angel.

CHAPTER 12: Dream Fields

Now, seriously, go on through before I blow you back to the winds. *Poof!*" A ball of fire shot from his mouth and *poof!* went Patsy! The dragon reared up declaring, "Heavens to Betsy!" and threw himself over the flaming creature to snuff her out.

After some time, Patsy wriggled out from underneath his belly, and when she emerged, she was a sorry sight to behold. Her wings were scorched, her face and hands were covered in soot, and her once-white feathered hair stuck up in short black spikes around her head.

When the dragon saw what he had done to the delicate little angel, his heart burst, which is saying something because this guy didn't even know he had a heart, much less that it could burst! He wept, sending a waterfall of tears down his cheeks, so many tears that he nearly drowned the poor blackened angel.

"You weren't supposed to get burnt," he snuffled. "I never burnt an angel in all my life. Does it hurt?"

"Yes, it hurts very much."

"Oh gosh, I'm so sorry. I never thought I had the POWER to burn an angel."

In spite of her burns, Patsy had to laugh. The mere act of the dragon's sobbing had caused the sky to crackle with lightning and the mountain to rumble and rock. "Why you're the most powerful being I've ever met," she said.

"I am? I just thought I was a big, useless ... well, you know, roadblock."

"Well, you're not. You're a Very Important Dragon. Maybe if you took your job more seriously, the other angels wouldn't think they were so indestructible."

"Oh? ..."

"Now may I please go through?"

"Of course. I beg your pardon." The dragon got himself out of her way, completely forgetting the test. Then he sank into thought, and that's how Patsy left him, all hunkered over at the edge of the road with his chin on his belly, thinking ... thinking.

Patsy made her way up the steep path. It wound round and round without ever seeming to go up. The scenery was always the same. Ahead, emerald green pine trees with soft translucent bristles. Above, blue cloudless sky. Below, many large fluffy white clouds, each a floating island with a temple nested in its center. After Patsy rounded the mountain the thirteenth time, she found herself standing before the shining White Palace where God lived. No one stood at the gate to greet her, so she let herself in through the big golden doors.

When Patsy entered the Divine Hall, she found herself completely in the dark.

CHAPTER 12: Dream Fields

Contrary to angelic lore, the Hall was not filled with pure white light, nor did God sit on a golden throne. There was no God to be seen at all. Only one simple flame burned in the center of the room. Patsy walked slowly towards it, and as she did she felt ... well, this may sound strange, but she felt as if a huge Ear were pressed to her heart, and the closer she got the more deeply the Ear heard.

"God?" she whispered.

"Uh-huh." The voice came from the same place as the Ear. She felt that she was in the presence of a very dear friend, not a great big impressive friend but a friend who was perhaps very small, like Cora, who had been waiting a long time to see her and had been very lonely in the meanwhile.

"I've come to find out what I'm supposed to be doing in heaven, God. I don't belong. I'm not like the others. I'm flammable."

"I know," said God. "So am I."

Then there was just silence, and listening, and a great deal of comfort passed between. Finally God whispered, "Angels are *meant* to be flammable."

Patsy wanted to tell God that most angels considered themselves to be non-flammable, and maybe if the dragon hadn't been sleeping on the job, there would be more flammable ones, but she decided to hold her tongue. She felt that she should perhaps not take up anymore of God's time, but she did have one more ... well, *burning* question to ask.

"God?"

"Uh-huh."

"How do I keep from going up in flames?"

God thought for a while and then said, "Imagine I am a collector of angels, and I have two angels that are very dear to me. One of them is delicate, old and handmade. The other one is a store-bought angel, made in a factory and indestructible. Which angel do you think I am going to be most careful with?"

"Well, the delicate one, of course."

"And so it is with you, Patsy. Stay flammable, just the way you are, and while you're out looking after others, I'll be looking after you."

It wasn't exactly the answer that Patsy was hoping for. She would have preferred some antidote for flammability, but it was a comforting response. She thanked God with all her heart, pulled herself away from that warm, intimate Presence, and made her way out of the Divine Hall.

CHAPTER 12: Dream Fields

Down the spiraling road she went. When she came around the last curve, there was the dragon, craning his head up the road. He offered to give her a ride back to her home cloud, and she gratefully accepted. He lifted her up, gently tucked her into the folds of his belly, and together they flew down through the tail of the winds.

The next day, Patsy the blackened angel sat with Cora on the steps of the angelic temple while the other greater angels got ready for work. Laughing, joking and carrying on, they streamed down the stairs and disappeared under white billowy clouds. Cora put a small wing around Patsy's charred back while she related the whole story. Afterwards they sat in silence, staring down into the clouds.

"So, are you ready?" Cora asked finally.

"As ready as I'll ever be."

They spread their wings and flew down towards the earth where fires broke out day and night—here, there and everywhere. Patsy started out very much afraid, but she trusted that God was looking out for her, and she flew straight down into the pain. Oh yes, she caught fire, but when she lit up, the most beautiful, compassionate angel would appear, and the person would feel so comforted that all the fires of pain would go out, sometimes for as long as forever. Patsy's wings never whitened, but no angel in heaven was more effective than her at dousing flames. Seeing this, the others stopped scorning her and began to wonder about the flammability of angels. As time went by, a few brave souls set off through the winds in search of their own flammability, which the dragon—who now took his job very seriously—made sure they found.

CHAPTER 12: Dream Fields

CHAPTER 12: Dream Fields

"The dragon lifted her up, gently tucked her into the folds of his belly, and together they flew down through the tail of the winds."

It's not going to be an easy story to illustrate, but like the dragon, I'm going to try to carry that angel down. It's an exhilarating challenge, though I'm already experiencing the winds of doubt. When something hasn't been done before, you meet the worst kind of resistance. I've been fighting a storm of voices inside that are telling me it's a ridiculous venture. There are reasons why no one has done this before. Who am I to think I can do it?

Still, "The Flammable Angel" is the story I want to tell. I e-mailed the author to ask permission to illustrate her story, and maybe take some license in drawing it out. She wrote back saying, sure go ahead, if you're true to the story you can tell it any way you wish. Now I'm staring at the story and wondering how I'm going to draw out God. What did I see when I heard the word "GOD"? It wasn't a guy with a beard. Can I communicate what I saw as "GOD"? Will others be able to recognize what I saw? It's a tall order but I want to dive down there and retrieve what I saw under my consciousness when I heard the story told.

I know I can do it. Maybe it comes from spending so much time doodling, letting pictures reel out from within.

But I have to say, the winds are fierce.

CHAPTER 13

Coming to Light

CHAPTER 13: Coming to Light

A Seeker's Journal

April 26

I've got all my materials set out, my drawing table is ready. I am prepared to draw. Now all I have to do is start. But I'm blocked. I wonder if I'm really good enough. I keep drawing other things, taking out my sketch pad, sitting in my chair, doodling, thinking about the story. It's like standing on the edge of the diving board. I can't jump.

Instead of drawing, I've been staying out late at night, after work, breaking my own policy, partying with the staff, deliberately doing things to distract me. Bruno Riccio had a showing at his gallery the other night, and I went with Caroline. Needless to say, I was looking less forward to seeing his work than being with Caroline.

It wasn't a positive experience. Caroline finally met this "god" (Yes, Albert, remind yourself that's "dog" spelt backwards) and she is attracted to him like every other healthy heterosexual woman would be. They've both got way more animal magnetism than any two people deserve. They were attracted to one another like two cats in a barn. I think he's dangerous—he's used to having everything he wants and moving on. I said as much to Caroline, and she said, "Yeah, I know, he's all wrong, but look at him, isn't he just so PERFECTLY wrong?" She strolled away. I proceeded to get drunk.

This distraction has not made it easy for me to concentrate. It has just raised a whole lot of dust. I'm struggling. I've been so pissed off and irritated in the last few days. Caroline hasn't called and I refuse to call her. It's ridiculous. We're friends. That's all, friends, and I'll do anything not to jeopardize that. But I've been in a funk for days. Then at night, in my sleep, I feel as though that little angel is coming down to visit, and pushing me. "C'mon Albert, you can do it. Bring me to light!"

May 3

Yesterday I decided I was gonna do it no matter what. For the angel. I didn't start at the drawing table. I made it easy on myself. I took out my sketch pad, went and sat in my usual spot by the window, and dove in. I'm no longer questioning myself. I've sealed out all forms of distraction, and taken two weeks off work to get primed. I've turned off the ringer on the telephone. I get up early in the morning and I draw. I go out for a ride on the bike. I come back in. I draw.

CHAPTER 13: Coming to Light

FROM THE DESK OF A. SEEKER

Years ago, I had tucked "The Oyster's Gift" away between books on my bookshelf. One afternoon, when I was looking for a distraction from the "job," I pulled a book off the shelf and this story fell out.

The Oyster's Gift

Down in the grassy sands of the sea, there lived an old oyster. He kept himself well hidden most of the time, in the shadows under the rocky overhang of a cave.

His presence wasn't entirely a secret, however. A mermaid in the area knew he was there. She had green eyes, a green tail and sea-green hair. She would come whirling like a wind through the high sea grasses and circle round the mouth of the cave. Mermaids go looking for oysters like him. They want the pearls. If a mermaid puts a pearl in her throat she can sing exquisitely.

"I know you have a pearl in there," she would whisper to the oyster. "Won't you open up and give it to me?"

But the oyster refused. "Nhhhhhhh uhhhh," he would say, locking his jaw. It wasn't that he didn't *want* to give the mermaid his pearl; he would give a thousand pearls to hear that legendary voice. His problem was, he wasn't sure he had a pearl to offer. Oh, he thought he might, he felt so nasty and irritable most of the time. But what if he opened up and the mermaid looked inside, and she saw nothing? Then what would he do? He didn't think he could bear the disappointment. She would swim away forever, leaving him to his shadows and his solitude, without so much as an excuse for his rotten disposition.

For her part, the mermaid believed in that cranky old oyster. Every day she came whispering, urging him to open up, but every day, the oyster refused. "Nhhhhhh uh," he would say, clamping his jaw down tight as tight could be. Lately the mermaid had become melancholy, and the oyster feared that one day she might lose hope and disappear forever.

How that thought distressed him! Night after night he sat awake, looking up through the sea at the wavering stars, hoping they would write some clue onto the surface as to the content of his own insides. Never had he felt so alone. But then one night, he realized something. He loved the beautiful mermaid, and so of course he would give her everything, even if he had nothing to offer! And that was that.

The next day, he waited with great anticipation for her to arrive. But she didn't. Instead, a diver came swimming by, and when he saw that fat old fellow sitting in the shadows under the rocky overhang of a cave, he scooped him into his bucket and swam to the surface.

There, the oyster was dumped into a larger bucket, and a larger one after that, and then into a bucket so vast that the oyster could see neither sky nor sea, only oysters in every direction. Then the group was divided and divided again, and at last he landed on ice under the twinkling golden lights of an oyster bar.

CHAPTER 13: Coming to Light

A huge man with a great moustache came by, along with his daughter, a meek teenage girl with a splash of freckles on her nose. Her father leaned over the ice and rubbed his hands together. "I'll have that big one over there," he told the chef, licking his chops. He turned to his daughter and caught her eye. "It'll be real GOOEY inside."

His daughter went to say, "Ewwwhh!" but she caught herself. She was deaf. She had never known the sound of her own voice, and she was terrified to make waves of any kind. She had chosen to remain silent, but lately she had been feeling so invisible that she thought one day she might disappear altogether.

"Tell you what," her father boomed. "If there's a pearl in that one, I'll give it to you."

Her cheeks flushed and her eyes widened as the chef shucked the oysters one by one until he came to the last. "Now for the grand-Daddy," he said. With great force, he pried it open, and out popped a huge pearl, as pink as the petals of the most delicate rose. It rolled across the cutting board.

"MINE!" hollered the girl. Flinging herself across the ice, she caught the pearl just as it reached the edge of the counter. It wasn't until she had it in her fist that she realized she was sprawling over the ice like a great fish amid oysters, lobsters and clams.

Her father laughed his big horsy laugh, and he helped her get back on her feet. The girl turned the pearl round and round under the golden lights, marveling at her gift from the sea. "Ooohhhh," she said, her voice flowing out over the beautiful treasure. "Ahhhhhhhh." Hearing the commotion, people in the restaurant left their tables and came crowding around. "Oooohhh," they said when they saw the pearl. "Ahhhhhhh." The girl was so caught up in the wonder of the pearl, she forgot her voice altogether and let it swim out like a fish into a stream. Soon after, she had the pearl made into a necklace and she wore it around her throat. From then on, she felt different somehow—more bubbly, more able to flow outward into the world of sound; never again so painfully shy …

And did I mention, she had sea-green eyes?

CHAPTER 13: Coming to Light

CHAPTER 13: Coming to Light

"I know you have a pearl in there. Won't you open up and give it to me?"

I know that mermaid swimming through the tall sea grasses. She's been with me through this whole period, prompting me to release the pearl. "Open up, Albert, open up." Who is she, this releaser of dreams?

On New Year's Eve, Caroline came over. I got the nerve to show her some of the work. She sat cross-legged on my living room floor and looked at the boards. I only gave her six or seven, about a hundred images. I expect there will be six or seven hundred by the time I'm finished.

She studied them for a long time and then she said, "I can read these Albert."

"Yeah?" I said, sitting on the sofa, feigning disinterest.

"Yeah. You want me to?" And so she started: "Once there was a little angel who lived on a high cloud in heaven. She was smaller than all the other angels and different. They had bright, glistening white wings, but her wings were short and spiked and ... burnt. The other angels looked down on her ..."

In that instant, it wasn't Caroline I saw sitting there cross-legged on the floor, reading the storyboard. It was Alison. Alison, the angel with the burnt wings, reading her own story out loud, from a book—maybe the only book in the world that she would ever be able to read.

I could feel the heat of tears on my face. I didn't ever want Caroline to stop. I never heard anything so beautiful as her voice as she labored to say what she saw and make sense out of it. She was so like Alison, so completely unaware of the purity of her self and the simple, childlike rhythm of her words. It was the most sacred of all moments.

"What happens next?" she asked. I was too overcome to answer. She put the boards down and came over to the sofa. We kissed. And then there was just silence ... and listening.

CHAPTER 14

Playing it Out

CHAPTER 14: Playing it Out

FROM THE DESK OF A. SEEKER

No journal entry this time. I was in a really creative place, completely swept up in the project. One afternoon I walked to work and this story literally came tumbling and sliding down the sidewalk towards me. Thank God it was stapled or the pages would have been all over the street. It didn't surprise me when I read the title:

"THAT Place"

I had arrived.

CHAPTER 14: Playing it Out

THAT Place

One night at sunset, a strange man came walking into town. He passed the grim workers who poured out of the factories. He passed school children dragging their satchels behind them. He passed women, burdened down with infants and groceries. He passed all the people who were trudging home, and walked into the center of town.

He arrived at a plain white fountain in the town square. His eyes searched the buildings around the fountain. He noticed a FOR SALE sign in front of an old red schoolhouse. As he watched the orange sun sink behind the silhouetted bell, a smile crept across his face. "It'll be THAT Place," he said.

The next day the man went to the mayor's office and he bought the schoolhouse for a bag of gold. The mayor, who was a generous fellow in every way, was pleased. He presented the key to the man, and welcomed him to town.

"Are you a school teacher?" the mayor asked.

"No," said the man. "I'm more of a ... playwright."

The mayor dropped his jaw. "What? You're going to turn the school into a PLAYhouse?"

"Yes, something like that," said the man.

"You won't arouse much interest for plays in Oldbones," said the mayor. "The people in this town are hard working. They have no time for plays."

"I wonder," said the man, making the key dance in the palm of his hand. Then he put it in his pocket and walked outside.

Now, the town of Oldbones was not a gossipy town. It was a town that kept to itself. Oh, occasionally it would open a tired eye or raise a work-worn brow, but generally it was a quiet town, a working town. It might read a book in the evening or play a game of cribbage with what was left of the day, but then it went to bed.

So Oldbones wasn't particularly interested in the strange man who came to town and bought the schoolhouse for a bag of gold. It didn't notice the sound of the hammer banging in the schoolhouse yard or its bright new coat of red paint. However, it did notice the sign that appeared out front on Wednesday night, which read: "Journey to THAT Place. Departure at 8."

The sign sent a ripple of curiosity through the town that mostly affected young people. On Wednesday night, two dozen young men and women stole away from hearths and cradles, mothers and fathers and cribbage tables. They hurried down dark cobblestone streets and disappeared into the red schoolhouse. The next

CHAPTER 14: Playing it Out

morning, they sat at their kitchen tables and announced to their fathers and mothers that they would not do their schoolwork. When they were asked why, they replied that the universe worked and they too would work, but only if the work worked, and their work did not.

Well, this kind of gibberish stunned the practical people of the town. "What do you mean?" asked an earnest mother. Her boy was prone to being carried away, but never so far as this. "What have you dreamed?"

Her son replied, "I've dreamed nothing, but I've been somewhere, to another place and time. You can go there too. Go to THAT Place and you'll see what I mean."

"Nonsense!" said his father coming into the kitchen. "You've been to the schoolhouse to see a PLAY."

"It wasn't a play," said the boy. "It was a voyage. We travelled to the other side of the universe in an interdimensional transportation device. We gathered at the meeting place of all living things."

"You sat in a schoolhouse that's been rooted to the ground for centuries!" roared his father. "It's got a bell on top, it's where people used to go to LEARN things."

"You went to school there, dear, when you were five," his mother echoed tearfully, wringing her hands.

"No, mother, it's—"

Bang! went the man's fist on the table. The cat sprang from the counter and the boy's mother wept. But all the knocking in the world would knock no sense into the boy, and eventually, like the other young people, the boy stayed home.

Oldbones was an experienced town, so it was only bemused by the truant children. Its humor vanished, however, when it woke up the next morning to discover that many more youngsters had gone to the playhouse the night before. They all came back insisting that the play was real and they too refused to do their schoolwork. They explained that the universe worked and they too would work, but only if the work worked, and their work did not.

"THAT Place is not real. It's a play!" cried their families, growing alarmed.

"But it IS real," said the youngsters. "And if you don't believe us, go see for yourselves."

Some people did. In fact, during the week that passed, nearly half the townspeople did. And when they returned from THAT Place, they too refused to work. Now Oldbones found itself in a very uncomfortable position. Working families became divided along the boundaries of those who had been to THAT Place and those who firmly remained in THIS Place.

CHAPTER 14: Playing it Out

Those who went to THAT Place recovered from their fatigue. They chatted enthusiastically among themselves, went walking along the country roads and painted the plain white fountain in the town square in ribbons of color.

Those who stayed in THIS Place were put under terrible pressure because they had to keep the town running with fewer and fewer people. After working a fourteen hour day, they trudged home and fought with their families until dawn. Some, out of sheer misery, gave in and went to THAT Place.

Finally, a party of fifty men burst into the mayor's office. They were led by a wiry, fiery man named McDermott. "Send the playwright packing or we'll burn the schoolhouse down!" he commanded.

The mayor assured the group he would talk to the man. The party waited in his office while the mayor went to the back of the schoolhouse and up the stairs to a tiny apartment where the playwright lived. The man came to the door, looking disheveled.

"I warned you," said the Mayor. "We don't want a disturbance in this town. If you want to stay, you'll have to explain your purpose here."

"Come in," said the man, kindly. He offered the mayor a chair. "What is it you would like to know?"

The mayor remained standing and cleared his throat. "Well first of all, what in God's name is THAT Place? And where is it? How do you get there? What is the mechanism of travel? Level with me, man. Is this a real experience or a play?"

"If the people say it is real, then it is real," said the man. "But if they say it is not real, then it is not real. They are the only ones who can judge. I will burn the place down myself if the townspeople wish me to. But in all fairness, they ought to see for themselves before they make a judgment."

The mayor considered the man's reasoning to be sound. He returned to his office where the men waited, buzzing like a hive of angry bees. In a booming voice he announced, "The man is prepared to go peacefully. But he won't be judged by a group of people who haven't seen his play. Before you judge him, go see his play."

The party broke up, disgruntled. Once again, they divided among themselves. Some went to see THAT Place and others adamantly refused. They knew that if they left THIS Place and went to THAT Place they wouldn't be able to return. And sure enough, the people who went to THAT Place came out of the schoolhouse saying that the universe worked and they too would work, but only if the work worked, and their work did not. Even the mayor went, and when he came back, he took a leave of absence.

CHAPTER 14: Playing it Out

Now, McDermott and the few who stayed in THIS Place decided to take matters into their own hands. In the middle of the night, they went to the schoolhouse, dragged the man out of his apartment and brought him to the town square. A crowd gathered as McDermott lit a torch and announced that he was going to burn the schoolhouse down.

The news rushed through Oldbones like an alarm. People poured out of their homes and went running to the town square. "What are you doing to the playwright?" they shouted. "Leave him alone!"

"The world needs practical people," said McDermott, stepping up to the fountain. "Our town was built on people who are willing to work hard. We need people who have their feet on the ground. We don't need dreamers with their wild inventions. If THAT Place is so real, then he can go back to it! He doesn't belong here!"

McDermott had a small but vigorous following, and they cheered for a good five minutes. When they had finally blown themselves out, a man came forward, took off his hat and said:

"I humbly suggest that you go to THAT PLACE and see what is possible. It's a better world than this weary old fact-grinding town, where we work like machines. Go to THAT Place. Then see how you feel about THIS Place."

Someone from McDermott's group yelled, "Kill the playwright!" and an ugly battle broke out.

The mayor was soon rustled out of his sleep by the anxious townspeople. They pleaded with him to settle the dispute. He rose at his own pace, put his clothes on, and strode into the center of town. He got up on the fountain and told the crowd to shut up. Then he addressed the playwright.

"What do you have to say to these people who are so terribly divided over your play? How will you mend the division between the people of this town?"

The man shook his head sadly, and he said, "They have missed the point."

"What does he mean?" whispered the crowd.

"What is the point?" the mayor asked.

"I can't tell you," said the man. "If you can't find it yourselves, then my work is useless. Give me the torch. I will destroy it myself."

The mayor turned to the crowd. "Well now, you've seen the play. What is the man's point?"

A man stepped forward. "The point is, THAT Place is more real than THIS Place, even if it is a play."

CHAPTER 14: Playing it Out

"Is that the point?" the mayor asked the playwright.

"No," he said. "That is not the point."

A woman shouted, "The point is, after being to THAT Place, we can no longer live in THIS Place."

"Is that the point?" the mayor asked.

"No," said the playwright. "That is not the point."

A young girl with a studious look came forward. With perfect elocution she said, "The point is, we have to find out where in the cosmos THAT Place is located, and then invent a mechanism for getting there."

"No," said the playwright sadly. "That is most definitely not the point."

One by one, the people who had been to THAT Place came forward. But the point appeared to be completely lost on them. Finally, McDermott handed the man his torch. "Seems your art ain't so hot dang special after all," he said. "Here, put a little reality to it."

The man took the torch. Full of resolve, he walked towards the schoolhouse. Oldbones followed, confused, teary and distraught. He threw the torch through a front window, and stood back as the schoolhouse began to burn.

Oldbones strained to see what was going on, its faces lined with concern. The town couldn't understand why he was putting the torch to his own work. It worried that it had missed something terribly important in missing the point.

Just then, a little girl came forward. She strode right up to the playwright and tugged the bottom of his coat. She stood firm, thrusting her hands deeply into the pockets of her striped overalls.

"It's okay, mister. It don't matter if the school burns down. You already showed us where to find THAT Place." She knocked her fist to her breast. "We got it in HERE."

The playwright smiled and tousled the girl's hair affectionately. Confounded, Oldbones stared at the playwright. McDermott scratched his head. A light, carefree breeze flirted with the hair of the people in the crowd, and the spirits of that old, work-worn town were lifted. As Oldbones began to consider THAT Place in its own heart, the effort the town had put into living began to melt away. One by one, bright visions and long-buried dreams were released like colorful balloons into the leaden sky.

Suddenly, the schoolhouse burst into flames. A flare of sparks shot up into the night air and showered the crowd in fireworks. The whole town cheered. Caps and coats flew into the air, children were raised on shoulders, and people jostled for a view of the burning school.

CHAPTER 14: Playing it Out

As for the playwright, his work was done. He picked up his bag and walked through the crowd. He saw the red light that flickered on the upturned faces of the men, women and children. He saw the water that glistened in their bright eyes, and the smiles that smoothed their lines. He walked to the edge of town, and disappeared into the night.

CHAPTER 14: Playing it Out

CHAPTER 14: Playing it Out

"The man came to the door, looking disheveled ...."

Like the playwright, I'm obsessed. I'm in for the long stretch. I have to see this to the finish. It's endurance I need now. And faith. I have the caption "Faith, the final frontier," written over my drawing table. There's whispering in certain quarters. Some of my friends think the book is a bizarre idea. They say I should go to school and learn more about animation before trying something like this. They want to know where the market is for the book.

They don't understand where the work is coming from. I'm the only one who can know THAT Place, and the more I believe in it and draw it out, the clearer it becomes. I wouldn't call this work "animation," it's illustration. I'm trying to illustrate a story without using words. I'm aware now that I've been pursuing this art form for a long time. Since I was young, my attention has been focused inward. I was a daydreamer, which I always thought was a bad thing. But in fact, all my life, I've been watching pictures come up from the inside. For the longest time I couldn't focus on those pictures, they would break up. I had to be unfocused, and let them arise naturally. In a word, doodle. But now that I know what's going on, I can cooperate with the process and not get in the way. I want to learn how to tell stories in pictures, and I'm finding out how to do that in a natural way, the way a child discovers the world.

My head is still crowded with thoughts of all the things I should be doing. The whole town of Oldbones is in there, resisting the playwright. I understand his discombobulation, but like him, I'm committed to drawing out THAT Place until the work is done.

I've asked quite a few people to read the boards. I listen for where they stumble. That's what I'm looking for. I want them to be able to flow with the story, to get the ideas without reaching so far they become frustrated. At the same time I want to give play to their imaginations and create lots of latitude for interpretation. That's the real work, and I have to stick with it. It's hard. It's taken me months to get it right, to find the flow.

People seem to like to read these images ALOUD. It's a challenge to read pictures, almost a game. Some people won't dare. There's a certain risk associated with trying to say what you see. But those who take the leap become like children and something sacred happens every time.

CHAPTER 15

The Big Test

CHAPTER 15: The Big Test

A Seeker's Journal

September 3

I flew home for Alison's birthday in August. I had mocked up the book and made a hand-colored copy for her. I wanted her to be the first to have it. I figured Alison's understanding of what I've done would be my biggest test. Would it work?

When I got home, I found out that Alison's having a rough time. Her group home supervisor was recently diagnosed with cancer and Alison's world is falling apart. Talk about the dragon of change. She's going to have to move to a new group home, adapt to a new supervisor, new roommates, even new work. It's all going to change at once. It took her years to learn the bus routes to get back and forth from the work shelter and earn that feeling of independence that is so crucial to her sense of self. Now she's going to have to start all over. She's had a lot of other serious challenges in her life, but at 39, Alison has never seen her world upturned. She's never experienced loss, illness or death.

She's scared. She wants to move home, which isn't possible. Mom and Dad are getting too old, plus she'll regress to the dependent child she was, and lose all the ground she has gained being on her own and working.

The night I arrived, Alison was sitting in her usual spot in the living room, at the far end of the couch, close to the lamp as she could be, cuddling up to it as though it were a flame. She looked more pale and withdrawn than usual. She has always been quite small, only about five feet tall. She has the most delicate features. She's got this fairy-like fragility about her—extremely delicate bones, and thick brown hair. Each strand as fine as a spider's thread.

After breakfast the next morning, I presented her with the package. I pushed it across the table to her and said, "Look Alison, I made you a present. It's a book that you can read."

She took it with interest and began to flip through it. "Oh, there's harps!" she exclaimed.

I forgot that Alison likes harps, she adores them. If she could have one wish, it would be to play the harp. It must be those long, sensitive fingers of hers. They look like they are just itching to play—as if, left to their own devices, they could play. She will sit and watch chamber orchestras on TV for hours in rapt attention.

"How many harps?" said Mom, leaning forward. "Oh look, angels! How many angels? Count the angels, Alison, count the harps."

CHAPTER 15: The Big Test

My heart sank as my great labor of love turned into a math quiz. Alison set to the task with enthusiasm, she flipped through the entire book looking for harps, which of course only belonged to the greater angels. She found six. She didn't seem to notice the little flammable angel at all.

CHAPTER 15: The Big Test

FROM THE DESK OF A. SEEKER

I heard this story, "Starry Eyes," on the radio after I got back home. I thought, Well, I guess I'm not the only one in the universe to get his hopes up, only to have them shattered.

CHAPTER 15: The Big Test

Starry Eyes

There is a boy who wants to come down from the stars. He is floating very near the atmosphere of the earth. For a long time he has been considering making a journey to the planet. His star friends are concerned that his plans might be too ambitious. But he keeps coming back to the edge of the atmosphere, each time with more and more conviction. He wants to bring the truth to the earth people. He wants to show them their place in the universe so they will not feel so lonely and lost. He believes that among the stars, he alone has been appointed to accomplish this task.

His friends in heaven know that he is a brilliant star with special powers. But they also know that the atmosphere of the earth is dense and that he could destroy himself in attempting to penetrate the planet's shell. He might even destroy the fragile globe.

The star boy is determined. He insists that he can protect himself and the earth. Using the power of his thought, he creates a crystal sphere around himself—transparent and light as a bubble. His fellow star beings follow the bubble as he floats down towards the earth. Again and again he tells them not to worry; he will survive his task. His eyes are bright and full of conviction, even as he passes into the atmosphere of the planet and his companions disappear into the night.

The bubble floats down, down, and all of a sudden there is an intense explosion in the sky. The next thing the boy knows, he is standing on a beach amidst fragments of glass so small that they mingle with the grains of sand. He kneels and tries to scoop up the sand but there is too much of it. Sheets and sheets of sand spread out on either side of him, as far as the eye can see. As his eyes adjust to the light, he sees the form of the green sea before him, the blue sky above him, the white sand around him and the dark forest behind. He stands up, his hands filled with sand, but he cannot hold it. The grains seep through his fingers. He cannot bring the world back inside. All the glory of what he knew is shattered.

Lonely and destitute, he makes his way along the beach, watching the gulls wheel and cry, knowing in his heart that now, in this place, he is no greater or lesser than a bird, a tree, a grain of sand. He is just another one of the multitude.

He looks out to sea, full of regret. It wasn't as if the stars didn't warn him that he would be destroyed. But is he destroyed? He looks at his arms, his hands, his legs, his feet. No, he is still alive. He is a fragment in a world where the truth has been shattered—yet every piece is true! So the star boy walks along the beach, empty in the belly of God—and in love with Everything.

CHAPTER 15: The Big Test

CHAPTER 15: The Big Test

*"The star boy walks along the beach, empty in the belly of God—
and in love with Everything."*

I was devastated that Alison didn't get the story. I spent three days at my parents' house, walking around like a zombie. If Alison didn't understand it, what was the point? I had lost the reason why I had done the book in the first place.

Like the star boy, I snapped out of it when I finally clued in to what was going on in the present. I saw that Alison was totally preoccupied with having to move. I noticed how she kept following my mother around everywhere, repeating again and again: "I'm not moving. I'm not moving, do you hear me, mother? I'm not moving. Do you hear?"

Yet in spite of that terror, she counted angels. She carried the book to the kitchen table every morning, hoping to find more harps.

On the plane home, I realized how attached I had become to one outcome. On some level I had decided that if Alison didn't see herself in the book, the whole project would fail. The fact is, Alison may never notice the flammable angel. Maybe the story will never speak to her or give her the recognition she deserves. So what's left? What was the effort all about?

I began to think about why I did the book in the first place. Fundamentally, it was the work that was in me to do. I wanted to create a picture book for adults, and I did it. Pursuing that dream made me feel truly alive.

Maybe the book didn't bring the kind of recognition I hoped for, but it led to many things I didn't even know I hoped for. It led me to dive deeply into myth and symbolism to discover aspects of myself I would never have otherwise found. It's taken me on a journey that has changed my relationship with myself and my work. Now that I have a concrete product, I've been showing it to all kinds of people. Like a key, it has been opening doors to discussions with educators, publishers, animators. It has virtually replaced my portfolio because it most truly expresses what I'm pursuing. I take it everywhere I go, planting seeds.

CHAPTER 16

Full Circle

CHAPTER 16: Full Circle

A Seeker's Journal

October 22

This just in: I got a letter from Cadwell this morning. Cadwell, can you believe it? He wants to make a proposition to me. I called Caroline, and she sounded mysterious. "It was his idea. Just consider it, that's all," she said.

What can Cadwell possibly offer me? I've been getting all kinds of propositions lately. A proposition to join an animation company. A proposition to do some drawing for a university research team investigating international symbols. A proposition to do storyboards for a commercial production company.

Once again, I'm clarifying wants and don't wants, but this time, I've got more concrete stuff to work with. I've already ruled out animation. I wouldn't mind doing commercial storyboards. There's good money in it. I could quit waiting tables. But the problem is, commercial work would be exhausting, and it would pull me away from my focus right now.

So what is my focus? Well, I'm not sure, but it has to do with drawing out universals. I'm leaning to the research job, it would be a great learning experience. But I don't feel in sync with the people on the team. They're doing this with corporate funding from advertising and the funders have a firm bottom line. They want to know how to package and promote products internationally without having to duplicate packaging costs. They're not interested in exploring how symbols can be used to communicate deeply or universally. There isn't much latitude ....

October 28

Cadwell was warm, which is one of the great unnatural wonders of the world. He came out to greet me in the waiting room, wearing a smile that he had to keep remembering to freshen up. Cadwell doesn't like me—to put it more accurately, he has a great distaste for me. I am so far beneath him. He's making all this effort because he wants to use me. The question is, for what.

We sat down in his office and he took a position at his round table instead of behind his desk, further discomforting himself.

"Caroline has told me you're a fine illustrator," he began. "She's taken the liberty of showing me some of your drawings. They're pretty good."

I assumed my old rock face.

CHAPTER 16: Full Circle

"I wasn't happy about having to dismiss you, but now that your real talents have been brought to my attention, I'd like to make you an offer, more in keeping with your abilities."

He paused. I said nothing. He continued. "We have a need in this department for an illustrator. Someone who can do many different kinds of things: storyboards, product illustration, adwork. It's a serious position, Albert, a full-time, permanent position, as secure as you can find in these times. With an excellent benefits package. The salary is 30% more than you were making before, which I think goes a long way to acknowledging your real merit."

I felt myself moving out of my rock shell into my own skin. I rose from the table. "Thank you for the offer, Mr. Cadwell," I said. "I appreciate your consideration. However, I'm going to have to turn you down, I'm afraid. I'm considering several other offers."

"Oh well, then," said Cadwell, getting up awkwardly. "Good luck, Albert."

"Thank you, sir."

I left him scratching his head, trying to figure out who the hell could provide Albert Seeker with a better package than the one he just put on the table.

CHAPTER 16: Full Circle

FROM THE DESK OF A. SEEKER

This story arrived in the mail after my meeting with Cadwell. It came in the form of a small, illustrated book, with a note from my father, saying: "Thought you would enjoy this book. Reminds me of you. Love, Dad."

CHAPTER 16: Full Circle

The Broad Mind

Once there was a thing called a broad mind. I can't tell you what kind of a thing it was, but I can tell you what it looked like. It had wings for flights of imagination, webbed feet for plunging into the depths of things, eyes that could see into the farthest galaxies, and arms that could embrace the whole wide world.

Now one day, this broad mind landed on a log by the river, where a child of the giants sat tying a fishing line. It shook out its wings in the afternoon sun, and then it flew up into the air. The child grabbed it in mid-flight. "Oh, look how fast you fly," he said. "Gee, I wonder how fast you run?"

The child of the giants carried the broad mind to a racing track and set it down at the starting line.

"Now, run," commanded the child. The broad mind flew up into the air. "No, no!" he said. "I didn't say FLY, I said RUN. You don't need wings to run. Those wings will just slow you down." So he pulled all the wings off the little broad mind.

Once again, he set the broad mind down at the starting line. But the broad mind didn't run. Instead, it began to wonder about the purpose of this race. And so it swam down, down, into the origins of the game. It had almost plunged out of sight when the child grabbed it back.

"No, no!" he said. "I didn't say PLUNGE into the depths of things, I said RUN. You don't need webbed feet to run. Those webs will just slow you down."

He cut the webs from between the toes of the broad mind. When the surgery was complete, the broad mind had a pair of feet with toes designed for pure speed.

He put it back on the racing track, and what do you know? The broad mind RAN! Fast as an arrow, it flew—past the finish line and into a field, past the field and into a gully, past the gully and into a meadow.

The child loped behind and snatched it up. "You're fast alright, but didn't you see the finish line?" Well now, the truth was, it couldn't see the finish line, because the broad mind's eyes were designed for long-range vision.

"Never mind, I'll teach you how to see," said the child. He carried the broad mind back to the track, and set it down at the starting gate. He made it run, and stopped it at the finish line. Then he picked it up and set it back. After hundreds of setbacks, the broad mind's eyes refocused on the short range goal. It could no longer see the galaxies, but no matter. This mind could race!

Finally, the big day arrived. The children of the giants gathered at the racing track, each with a broad mind in a little cage. They set their minds down on the track and *bang!* a shot was fired. Out of the gates they sprang, and they ran as fast

CHAPTER 16: Full Circle

as they could to please their masters, but ours ran faster and it won the race! Oh, it was so delighted with its accomplishment, so pleased with itself and life, that it hugged the giant child, and then it hugged all the other children too. That was a mistake, for the giant children laughed at their friend. In turn, the giant scolded the broad mind. "You're not supposed to embrace everyone," he said. "You're only supposed to embrace ME." And then he shortened the arms of the broad mind.

Now, when the broad mind had its arms shortened, it didn't have such a great desire to race. It didn't win the second race, nor the third, nor fourth. The child stuffed the broad mind in his pocket and headed home. On the way, he threw it into a garbage can. "This mind is no use to me," he said.

The broad mind landed on a heap of others who, like him, had been thrown away. These poor used broad minds lived in a sorry state. There they were, grounded, without depth or imagination, unable to see the stars or even embrace one another. They tried to make the best of it in their container world, but it was a gray and colorless place.

After a while, the broad mind found that its wings were growing back. It hid the fact, because it was embarrassed by their glorious iridescent pinks and greens.

But then one day, while sitting on a bottle cap, when no one else was in sight, it shook out its wings to have a look. And what do you know, it took flight! It flew higher and higher until it could see the place where the giants lived. Much to its surprise, it found that the giants lived in a giant container. It flew higher and higher, beyond the container, only to find that the giant container was also contained by greater giants who lived in their own container. And so it went on, infinitely.

The broad mind floated down, down, and came back to its post on the bottle cap. Then it began to think. It sank down into the container until it had gone so deep that the webs returned to its toes. It plunged deeper and deeper into the meaning of containers until they meant nothing at all, and it surfaced free. Once again, it could see beyond the galaxies, and its happiness was so great that it flew around the whole world, leaving a shower of joy in its wake.

It landed on a log by the river, where a child of the giants sat tying a fishing line. The child made a grab for the broad mind, but this time the mind was smarter, and it flew away.

"Drat," said the giant child. "That one was a winner. How come the winners always get away?"

CHAPTER 16: Full Circle

CHAPTER 16: Full Circle

"Its happiness was so great that it flew around the whole world, leaving a shower of joy in its wake."

I ended up refusing all the offers. They were all wrong, each for their own reasons. Even Caroline said, "Aren't you being a little bit picky?" The answer is, yes I am. It's sharpening my senses. I'll know the right offer when it comes along, and meanwhile, I'm refining my waiting skills.

A couple of days ago, Mom called. She updated me on Alison's situation. She has moved to a new group home, and she's coping the best way she can, but she's having trouble sleeping, and often breaks into fits of anger or tears. Mom said she took Alison shopping last week and Alison saw a carved ebony angel in the window. She couldn't take her eyes off it; had to have it. Mom asked her, "What do you want that for?" and Alison blurted out, "Because she can hear my heart."

I was in a highly emotional state when I put the phone down. Right away, I called the local branch office of an association that works on behalf of people with intellectual disabilities. The number had been sitting on my desk for a while, as I had been thinking about doing volunteer work for them. I asked if they were offering any art classes, and if a volunteer artist might be helpful. The woman I spoke to, Marla was her name, sounded enthusiastic and we arranged to meet.

She was a radiant middle-woman with white-blond hair and a peaches and cream complexion. I showed her "The Flammable Angel" picture book, and she looked it over with interest. She took a lot of time, which pleased me. She was rather flushed when she put it down. "Good work," she said. "You've got a real gift for illustration." Then she asked me why I wanted to teach art to kids with disabilities.

I began to tell her about my sister. And suddenly, I was speaking so eloquently I surprised myself! I told her how important it was for me to reach children with special needs, and understand what was inside them. I talked about how art is a way of communicating that bypasses abstract intellectual thinking and goes straight to the heart, which has its own intelligence. I said, "I want to explore that innate intelligence, draw it out, go beyond barriers of intellectual ability." To demonstrate, I took out my sketch pad and I drew an oval. I said, "Here's a seed. Or maybe it's an egg. There's something inside it." I gave her my sketch pad. "What would you say it is?"

She looked at it, and she said, "It's a seed."

"What's inside the seed?" I asked.

CHAPTER 16: Full Circle

She said, "Hhmn. It's a flower, I think."

"What kind of flower?"

"A rose." About that, she was definite.

"Would you draw it for me?"

She laughed. "You're the artist! I can't draw."

I rifled through my pack for some colored pencils and markers, and put them on the table. I said, "Just approach this as if you were a child." Then I asked her to tell me about the rose, starting with its location. "Where does it grow?"

"All I can see is white," she said. "Oh, then I guess it's snow. It's growing in a garden where the snow hasn't finished melting. But I can't draw snow! For that matter, I can't draw a garden!"

I started coaching her. She found that she could draw more easily if she knew what it was she wanted to draw. So we spent most of our time defining the rose, its character, the way it grew, its stage of growth, its color and shape and size. What she couldn't draw, I showed her how to draw, and every now and then, I drew something for her. Throughout, we were focused on bringing her rose to light; not on how it was being drawn, or even who was drawing it. The point was to see her rose exactly as she saw it in her mind's eye.

In the end, there it was: a gorgeous, young, pale pink rose growing bravely all by itself in a garden that hadn't yet awakened to the spring. It took no prompting at all for her to tell me its story.

"It looks so fragile, doesn't it? But it's strong. It's been growing courageously—just fought through a bitter winter, and now it's blooming!" She laughed. "That's me! That's exactly how I feel!" We looked at the picture for a long moment. "Can you do this for everyone?" she asked.

I told her about all the years I had spent "doodling" and how it had led me to become conscious of the pictures we see unconsciously. I expressed my fascination with the unfolding worlds within us, and how important it is to recognize them—especially for people like my sister who isn't known to others or to herself. Within each of us there is some beautiful seed waiting to burst and grow.

Marla was glowing as I spoke. She said, "The District Public School Board is looking for an artist to work with youth who have special needs. They want to explore artistic approaches to learning where cognitive ones don't work. There's not much money in it. But that's where I think you should be—working with special needs teachers in the schools, learning from them, sharing what you know." She offered to call them and give me a referral.

CHAPTER 16: Full Circle

I took the subway home, my head humming with ideas and new possibilities. Finally, I had a sense of direction and I knew that wherever this journey took me, I would be home.

I settled in for the ride. I felt completely present in the moment, clear-minded and undistracted, just another one of the many people riding home on the subway, speeding along towards their destinations. The moment seemed to hang there, suspended, as though someone from another dimension had looked in and captured the scene in a photograph.

An elderly Oriental woman sat across from me with her hands calmly folded on her lap and a brown shopping bag at her feet. She wore a dark green raincoat and a transparent kerchief over her head. Our eyes met and she smiled warmly, as if we shared some special secret. The subway stopped. She reached for her paper bag and stood up. She couldn't have been more than four feet tall. The people who were crowded at the exit doors made a passage for her, as if she were royalty. "Who is she?" I wondered as she disappeared through the door.

And then it struck me. Of course! Old Mrs. Chang.

END

EPILOGUE

One last note. Alison's angel must have been listening, because she has found another home. Under the new system, clients are given more opportunity to choose the living conditions they want, and what Alison wanted most of all was to continue living with her roommate Sherry. They found a new home, closer to work, with a supervisor who also happens to be a sculptor. They do crafts on the weekends, and it seems that Alison has discovered clay ... I wonder what she'll make!

About the Author

Michelle Tocher is a storyteller and author of six books, including the celebrated book, *How to Ride a Dragon: Women with Breast Cancer Tell their Stories*, (Key Porter, 2001) Her books, workshops and websites focus on helping people to access their creative imagination as a source of hope and wellness.

With Masters degrees in Journalism and the History of Science, she is also author of *Brave Work: A Guide to the Quest for Meaning in Work*, first published by the Canadian Career Development Foundation.

For more information about the author, visit michelletocher.com, or explore her self-study program at wonderlit.com.

About the Illustrator

Richard Leach is an award winning graphic designer, design consultant, illustrator and fine artist with over 30 years of experience in the communications industry. Since his recent move to Prince Edward County, Ontario, Richard has been concentrating on fine art and describes his allegorical mixed media work as "the joyful assembly of diverse elements in a meaningful arrangement." He does giclée prints and relief on wood in either acrylic or encaustic mediums.

Richard holds a BA in Art Education from the University of Toronto and a Diploma in Art and Design from Sheridan College. He also completed two years of study in Fine Arts at Hornsey College of Art in London, England.

creative-edge-design.com

www.ingramcontent.com/pod-product-compliance
Lightning Source LLC
Chambersburg PA
CBHW041831300426
44111CB00002B/50